Contents

American Association of Collegiate
Registrars and Admissions Officers
One Dupont Circle, NW, Suite 520
Washington, DC 20036-1135

Tel: (202) 293-9161 | Fax: (202) 872-8857 | www.aacrao.org

For a complete listing of AACRAO publications, visit www.aacrao.org/publications/.

The American Association of Collegiate Registrars and Admissions Officers, founded
in 1910, is a nonprofit, voluntary, professional association of more than 9,500 higher
education administrators who represent more than 2,500 institutions and agencies
in the United States and in twenty-eight countries around the world. The mission of
the Association is to provide leadership in policy initiation, interpretation, and imple-
mentation in the global educational community. This is accomplished through the
identification and promotion of standards and best practices in enrollment management,
information technology, instructional management, and student services.

LIBRARY OF CONGRESS CATALOGING-IN-PUBLICATION DATA

Guide to bogus institutions and documents/American Association of Collegiate Registrars
and Admissions Officers.

p. cm.

ISBN 1-57858-072-2

1. Diploma mills—United States.
2. Student records—Forgeries—United States.
3. Authentication—United States.

I. American Association of Collegiate Registrars and Admissions Officers.

LB2388.G84 2005
378.2—dc22
2006014727

Introduction

"Is there one big book with a complete list of diploma mills, fake accreditors, bogus evaluation services and phony transcript vendors?" The answer, of course, is "No." The world of *fraud* is a dynamic one, populated by entities and individuals who adapt like chameleons and constantly reinvent themselves to do whatever is necessary to "make a fast buck." The problem of bogus universities and degree fraud has no "one size fits all" solution, and no "one" list or book could ever be exhaustive or completely up-to-date.

AACRAO presents this volume as a guidebook to give you the information and tools that you need in order to face and fight the complex battle against this type of fraud. This book will inform you about the issues, help you to learn techniques to detect bogus institutions and documents, offer guidelines in handling cases of fraud, help you to prevent your institution or organization from becoming a victim of fraud, and give you confidence in discussing all of these issues with colleagues and superiors.

The material in this book offers perspectives from the higher education, security, consumer protection, government, and law enforcement sectors, and ranges from general considerations of academic fraud, with working definitions that provide a practical basis for further investigation, to specific problems and cases covering a spectrum of the types of fakery found in higher education today. Some of these writings have appeared in AACRAO resources such as AACRAO's quarterly journal *College and University* and the *AACRAO Transcript*, while other works are original or reprinted with permission.

AACRAO wishes to thank the following colleagues who have contributed to this compilation, and whose invaluable and generous support of AACRAO's work on the issue of higher education fraud includes presenting at AACRAO conferences and workshops, as well as information sharing, research, and writing:

- ◆ **John Bear**, independent consultant, authority and expert witness on non-traditional education and diploma mill fraud, author of Ten Speed Press' *Bear's Guides* on alternative means of earning degrees, including information on bogus entities, and co-author with Allen Ezell of *Degree Mills: The Billion-Dollar Industry That Has Sold Over a Million Fake Diplomas* (Prometheus Books, 2005).

- ◆ **Allen Ezell**, retired FBI agent in charge of the 1980's diploma mill sting operation "DipScam," currently head of the corporate fraud division of Wachovia Corporation, and co-author with John Bear of *Degree Mills: The Billion-Dollar Industry That Has Sold Over a Million Fake Diplomas*.

- ◆ **Alan Contreras**, Administrator of the Oregon Office of Degree Authorization, expert on government interface with the higher education sector and regulatory action against purveyors of substandard and bogus "degrees."

- ◆ **Jane Yahr Shepard**, International Admission Manager, Office of Admissions, University of Wisconsin-Madison, and chair of the AACRAO International Publication Advisory Committee (IPAC), author, and conference presenter on country educational systems and best practices.

The following AACRAO staff members, all known for their interest in and commitment to fighting higher education fraud, have also contributed work to this volume:

- ◆ **Eva-Angela Adan**, AACRAO International Education Services special consultant, leader in international admissions, foreign credential evaluation, and professional development, author, and well-known presenter on bogus credentials.

- ◆ **Edward Devlin**, retired AACRAO Director of Special Projects and Monterey Peninsula College international programs director, life member of NAFSA, author and editor of several international admissions publications, leader in professional development activities.

◆ **Ann M. Koenig**, Southwest regional director with AACRAO International Education Services, author, researcher, committee member, national and international presenter on country educational systems, best practices in international admissions and foreign credential evaluation, and diploma mill fraud.

◆ **Jessica Montgomery**, contributing author to AACRAO's weekly news source *AACRAO Transcript*, covering federal relations, court proceedings, compliance and industry developments affecting higher education, with special interest in news about international education and higher education fraud.

◆ **LesLee Stedman**, Northwest Regional Director with AACRAO International Education Services, AACRAO coordinator of the annual Baden-Württemberg Seminar, frequent contributor to AACRAO news publications, and conference and workshop presenter.

◇◇◇◇◇◇◇◇◇◇◇◇◇◇◇◇◇◇◇◇◇

CHAPTER ONE

Why Verification of Suspicious Foreign Records Is Important

by Edward Devlin

There are many flags that might alert an international admissions officer to the possibility of fraudulent, altered or misleadingly-translated documents, including academic records, test results, letters of recommendation, and financial documents from countries known to have a high incidence of fraudulent documentation.

So why should an institution bother to get verification of documents? Isn't it enough that the admissions officer can figure out what something probably means, or that *surely* a visa won't be issued if the visa officer is suspicious about a document? What is the harm in admitting a student with altered documents anyway?

The answers fall into three categories: ethical, legal, and practical.

Ethical Considerations

The ethical imperative for verification is simple enough. If a school admits students on the basis of suspicious or incomplete documentation, and denies students admission on the basis of substandard but real documents, the result is the wholesale encouragement and reward of fraud. Simple fairness requires that a school take reasonable care to make sure that its admission and transfer credit practices reward only real achievement. Good practice demands that, insofar as possible, international students are held to the same standards as would be applied to domestic students.

On an individual level, it has become common practice in many countries to sell bogus documents, from marksheets and transcripts to complete degree dossiers. These are sold for anywhere from three hundred dollars (or less) to several thousand dollars in local equivalent currency. The Immigration and Naturalization Service (INS) I-20 form, which is issued by U.S. institutions to admitted applicants who wish to apply for an F-1 student visa, is especially sought after. One single I-20 form from a U.S. institution that is not careful about document review and admits a student based on fraudulent documents, can be reproduced and sold indefinitely. Obviously, most people who buy these will not be granted student visas, but having purchased fake documents, they are not in a position to complain to authorities.

The visa offices of many U.S. embassies and consulates are under tremendous pressure due to volume and limitations on resources. (For example, this author was recently told by a U.S. State Department official in India that two windows in the consular office in Mumbai were responsible for 300,000 in-person interviews and decisions each year!) In such circumstances, despite the rigorous training and dedication of consular officials, it is quite possible for a mistake to be made regarding the issuance of an F-1 visa. And, again, once word gets out that a "student" obtained such an entry document with a certain institution's I-20 form and "purchased" application support materials, that institution can shortly expect a flood of fraudulent applications.

To condone or ignore this fraudulent activity by not seeking verification of suspicious documentation is a clear violation of the partnership with the U.S. government that the institution has undertaken by applying for and receiving the right to issue I-20 forms. It is an ethical abdication that has both legal and practical consequences as discussed below.

Legal Considerations

The legal issue is also straightforward, particularly in the case of F-1 students. In completing an INS form I-17 to gain permission to accept international students, an institution is signing a legal document that requires it to meet INS guidelines, on penalty of losing permission to accept F-1 students should those requirements not be met. Each I-20 form that is issued states that the school has verified academic eligibility and financial sufficiency and is signed by an official designated on the I-17 or I-17A form. In other words, accepting F-1 students places a burden on the institution that must be taken seriously.

Practical Reasons

The practical reasons for verification are also rather clear-cut, although the interpretations may be more subtle and have long-lasting ramifications for the reputation of an individual institution's international admissions and student services.

On a macro level, if institutions permit suspicious or incomplete documents to be the basis for admission of international students, the reputation of U.S. higher education suffers worldwide. There is a distinct degradation of interest on the part of very good students to study in an educational system which is known to be naive; why should an honest and excellent international student want to study in the U.S. if applicants can be admitted to U.S. schools without earning their admission? Certainly Britain, Canada, Australia and other countries are eager to have those honest, excellent students, too.

The same warning applies more obviously to an individual institution. The reputation of an institution as an "easy mark" for questionable application documents is a hard one to repair. Once this reputation is public, good students will stay away. Weak ones will apply, fraudulently or not. As a single example, during the Iran hostage crisis, schools that did not seek verification suddenly had hundreds of unexpected transfer students. When the INS cracked down, the students all disappeared or were detained. The reputation of those schools took a very long time to rebuild. Many of the international student programs involved have never completely recovered.

Additionally, once word gets out (and it now travels at the speed of light) that a school is a "patsy," the number of fraudulent applications will skyrocket. At best, the consequences of admitting students who have misrepresented themselves—if indeed their intention is to study and they actually enroll at the institution—have to be managed using resources that the institution would rather use in much more constructive and positive ways.

Good Practice = Safe Practice

To safeguard the academic, ethical and legal authenticity of our institutions, as well as to continue to attract quality international students who contribute to the vitality, diversity, and quality of the U.S. higher education arena, it is imperative that we follow principles of best practice in the admission of international students. This means that international admissions professionals should have the training and resources they need to make sound professional judgments about the documents that applicants submit, that they receive the encouragement and support of enrollment managers to seek verification of suspicious documents, and that they share the results of the verification process with their colleagues. There is too much at stake to disregard or fall short on our responsibilities in this area.

◇◇◇◇◇◇◇◇◇◇◇◇◇◇◇◇◇

CHAPTER TWO

The Forensics of Academic Credential Fraud Analysis and Detection

by Eva-Angela Adán

"You are never aware of how little you know until you realize how much is there to be discovered"—these famous words I heard long ago are still resonant in my mind. They keep reminding me that even though I am not a scientist, the professional world in which I operate has been redefined by researching the obvious to investigating the questionable, the unexplainable and the unknown. It has expanded from the traditional research and analytical exercise of determining the comparability and placement of foreign academic credentials to the investigative task of a sleuth: the investigation of legitimacy. I am thankful to my childhood readings of Sherlock Holmes, which instilled in me the curiosity of looking beyond appearances! This is what the daily task of international credentials analysts or international education professionals calls for, no matter where they are in the world. They balance the act of fairly assessing legitimate academic credentials and qualifications while identifying both the obvious and the skillful deceits flooding the market today. Where these deceits are coming from is not a mystery, but one thing is certain—keeping track of the innovative ways illegitimate documentation continues to evolve is a daunting task. For college personnel in U.S. academic institutions and for professional credential analysts all over the world, the detection of fraudulent and illegitimate documents is a constant challenge and not as elementary as Holmes used to remind his long time partner Watson.

Taking into account the investigative road we have taken in this new area of academic credential analysis, a carefully designed methodology or quasi-scientific examination should be considered. This is an effective and reliable approach to analyzing and establishing the legitimacy of documents, beyond the initial reaction that something is wrong (which in many cases is the start of a long journey to uncover the truth). Such an approach allows analysts to conduct a transparent review of the elements physically identified as potentially questionable, and lead to evidential confirmation of fraud and/or verification of legitimacy. This should clearly convince all involved, including the culprit, that the findings derived from the examination of facts are more than a mere opinion, and that the likely analysis of facts by others would conclude with the same results (Hilton 1993, p. 11).

Illegitimate Credentials: What, Where, and Why

◆ **What?** The dark and hidden path of fraudulent and illegitimate academic documentation is extensive. It includes international academic credentials altered in a variety of ways, from a simplistic whiteout to a sophisticated creation produced in-house by college personnel in some countries, to even identical reproductions of legitimate international diplomas and transcripts, in some instances, created within the u.s. A recent product on the market is the instant educational gratification invented by the rapidly growing "Diploma Mill" industry. These are American-style documents (transcripts, diplomas and related documentation) manufactured, mass-produced and sold to the public.

◆ **Where?** Traditionally, altered international credentials come from countries where public corruption, and political instability are fertile ground for such illicit activities. They have been considered a "legitimate excuse" for individuals coming from war-torn countries and dictatorial regimes where it was not always possible to secure legitimate documents. Having their documents "recreated by market educational experts" and "appropriately designed" for foreign export is not considered inappropriate in the minds of many. As for "diploma mills" products, they can be openly purchased on the Internet, through magazine advertisements, and by dialing 1-800-numbers.

◆ **Why?** In today's world, an emerging public with the desire to gain quick access to postsecondary or tertiary education (inside and outside their native territory), and in search of better professional opportunities and higher pay, are increasingly contributing to the traffic of illegitimate documentation and products acquired through the carefully marketed campaigns of the "diploma mill" industry. This has all been made possible by the advances in modern technology, which, while expediting the analytical and investigative work of international credential analysts, has also facilitated the fast production and advertising of illegitimate academic documents worldwide. Opportunities for fraud are currently being enhanced by economically accessible technology that includes laser printers, easy-to-program type fonts and designs, color photocopying, scanning devices, and easy access to academic information through web-based catalogs and institutional web pages, which, in some cases, may include the signature of institutional officials, ready for scanning, copying and reproduction.

The unfortunate reality is that unawareness of the problem—by both employers and educators—and lack of knowledge about the variety of illegitimate documents on the market are allowing these products, with their inherently growing consequences, to impact all aspects of society: economics, education and the general welfare of the public.

Fraud and Illegitimate Documentation

The definition of fraud, according to the Columbia Electronic Encyclopedia (2004), includes the willful misrepresentation or alteration of a written document (*e.g.*, changing information, inserting new information or appending someone else's signature) to deceive others. This misrepresentation may include a lie as well as failure to disclose information; it is never considered the result of an accident or negligence because of its intended purpose. In the United States, forgery in its many manifestations may be considered a state or federal crime.

Based on the possible definitions given by the American Heritage® Dictionary of the English Language: Fourth Edition (2000), an illegitimate document is simply one similar in appearance to a genuine one but lacking validity. This description fits the reality of the bogus credentials produced by "diploma mills."

Therefore, for the purpose of this paper, one can define a legitimate and valid document as one issued and forwarded by the official bona fide authority in the traditional format and paper, and containing the appropriate seals or stamps and signatures. In addition, in the case of academic transcripts, they should reflect a study program typical of the educational system that it represents and degrees should have the official validity accorded by national academic and professional authorities overseeing the issuance of academic degrees and diplomas. Any document that does not meet these characteristics should be routinely rejected and/or subject to verification.

Types of Fraud

Based on the aforementioned definition one can identify five basic types of illegitimate or fraudulent documents in international credential analysis:

- ◆ **Altered Documents** are official, legitimate documents that have been altered through omissions, additions, or changes. These alterations may include, but are not limited to, changes in the date of birth, dates of attendance, initial enrollment and graduation dates, grades, curricular content, etc.
- ◆ **Fabricated Documents** (also known as counterfeit documents) are created to represent a legitimate or fictitious institution, and/or program.
- ◆ **Manufactured In-house** are documents produced by institutional representatives. These include both *altered* and *fabricated* documents in the national language or the language of the receiving country and designed "specifically for foreign consumption." In many cases, grades are inflated; contact hours or credits are doubled, and professional titles or degrees are awarded for programs that represent completion of only a partial or intermediate qualification.
- ◆ **Diploma Mills** produce bogus products (transcripts/diplomas) that although not defined as a fabrication, the study or qualification they claim to represent is illegitimate.
- ◆ **Interpretative Translations** are inaccurate translations of documents which are interpretative in nature and systematically misleading. Samples

include the well known (and often unintentional) literal translation of the Latin American high school diploma of *bachiller* into bachelor's, the conversion of grades into the U.S. grade scale A–F, and the translation of course titles to comparable subjects in the receiving country to enhance the possibility of transfer credit.

Other misrepresentations and types of fraud not covered in this article include false bank statements, bogus bank drafts, false letters of recommendation, altered or fraudulent test scores, and bogus or altered official documentation (such as passports, birth certificates etc. usually requested to verify the identity of a credential holder when age discrepancy is a defining factor).

Where do I begin?

The road map for a quasi-scientific approach to credential analysis and fraud detection begins with four basic questions:

① *Do I have all the documents I need to assess the academic qualifications of an individual?* Always review and compare the self-reported educational history or ladder with the documents received to determine any gaps in educational progression, and whether anything is missing. This should help the analyst establish what documentation is needed to have a complete academic profile. This may include school leaving examinations, certificates, academic transcripts (always use the indigenous terminology to request them) or examination sheets showing all courses attempted and completed, certificates or diplomas earned, and course descriptions if you need to determine the level of studies for transfer credit purposes. Arranging all documents in chronological order should also help the analyst determine if it all fits into the specific academic structure, *e.g.*, English, French, etc.

② *Do they make sense chronologically and structurally?* First and foremost, never fail to compare biographical data (date of birth, complete names, and gender) on all documents to make sure that "vital" elements match the person whose application is under review. In some countries, the national identity card number appears routinely on many official records, including transcripts. Checking this data element and including it in any verification inquiry could expedite the verification process. All these data elements are important when verifying the authenticity of a document and establishing the rightful owner.

When reviewing all the documentation submitted (*e.g.*, applications, examination certificates, transcripts, certificates/diplomas, recommendation letters, etc), make sure they fit chronologically into the progressive path of the individual's academic life. The educational chronology should be logical, both in terms of the system and the individual's age. Sometimes, a mismatch between birth, high school graduation and college entrance dates is a clear sign that fraud has been committed.

For example, I recall working a case in which a letter of recommendation, indicating asynchronous attendance dates, revealed that a student had never enrolled at the institution; the professor praising his glorious accomplishments had never taught him; and, the diploma held was the workmanship of an unscrupulous university administrator.

Any gaps in the educational progression of the individual should be justifiable, *e.g.*, academic failure, socio-political disruptions due to military service, university strikes (very common in some countries), wars, natural disasters, etc. These external circumstances that control the fate of a person's education can also allow you to uncover powerful evidence. For instance, an individual claiming graduation from an Afghan university presented a university diploma issued in January of 1980. Historically, this is considered an impossibility because the Russians invaded Afghanistan in December of 1979, and the country's educational activities resumed under the Soviet regime later on.[1] This continues to be a relevant issue today.

The realities of war and socio-economic devastation make it virtually impossible to identify a reliable source to verify academic documentation. However, knowledge of world affairs and educational developments will help you identify documentary anachronisms, such as diplomas with old university names, unchanged country names (*e.g.*, former Soviet republics), historically outdated country emblems (*e.g.*, Polish national emblem), etc. A recent exercise to verify the degree offerings of the University of Yaoundé II in Cameroon revealed that the transcript was fraudulent. The University of Yaoundé was divided into Yaoundé I and

---

[1] The current situation in Afghanistan was clearly described in an article written by Herman de Leeuw for the *ADSEC Newsletter* (08/25/06). An article by the same author appeared in April 2004 on the International Education Research Foundation Web site explaining the situation with the Kurdish Autonomous Zone of Iraq.

Yaoundé II in 1993; and the program/degree presented to me could not have been completed prior to the establishment of Yaoundé II.

Most helpful in this process is knowing educational benchmarks and how each document stacks up structurally in the educational ladder. This is particularly helpful when you are confronted with "transient scholars" who present documents generated through different educational systems. In a recent case, an applicant presented a certificate of completion of lower secondary education and a degree of *Licenciado* from a national university in the Latin America. The student's explanation was that the university had made an exception at the time and students were allowed to enter and complete a university degree without completing secondary school. The university confirmed that the alleged degree/titulo had not been issued.

Do they appear legitimate and show no manifestations of fraud attempts? Looks can be deceiving and this is especially true when dealing with "diploma mill" products and other types of bogus credentials. They are the perfect picture of the impeccable academic record but their educational value is only worthy in the eyes of the uneducated beholder. It is important for credential analysts to know the national system of the country they are dealing with and to become familiar with the various types of documents generated by the system to establish the legitimacy of a document: seals, language, emblems, their proper place in the record, etc. A closer look at a credential I recently examined from Cameroon revealed that the university crest had been scanned and super imposed on a plain piece of paper on a mirror image. Besides missing minor details lost in the process of replicating the seal, the words commonly appearing underneath the crest could only be read if you inverted the document. Small details like that make or break a perfect picture.

Transcripts are sometimes given the "original look." A transcript from the University of Liberia although signed with original ink (which I managed to test), did not feel like the traditional embossed seal, which you can easily test: place a blank piece of paper over the transcript and with a #2 lead pencil lightly rub over the seal. A "negative" of the seal will appear on the blank paper. The test failed. The transcript presented to me was a very poor attempt at an extreme make-over.

The issue of institutional recognition is of high importance, especially in the case of bogus credentials from "diploma mills." The appearance of the document is deceiving so the logical approach to determine its authenticity is to ask the next question.

◆ *Have they been issued by appropriate and legitimate authorities recognized within the national education system?* It is important to remember that, both in the U.S. and in most other countries, there are official resources listing postsecondary institutions accredited, recognized and authorized by legislative decrees to grant university-level degrees. This information should help determine if the documentation under review represents a "diploma mill" product, an unrecognized institution or degree, or a bogus credential endorsed by the wrong ministerial authorities. Analysts must be aware of which body is responsible for authorizing institutional recognition, program offerings, and degree awards. Generally, in centralized educational systems outside the United States, a central ministerial authority is in charge. For a list of ministries of education outside the U.S. visit the UNESCO web site: www.unesco.org/education/partners/mined/mined. htm. Direct links to ministries of the Sub-Sahara nations appear on www. ibe.unesco.org/links/southsahara.htm.

When reviewing transcripts and diplomas, it is important to remember that not all institutions/studies are recognized entirely by a ministry of national education. In some countries, specialized institutions/studies such as health, agriculture, and military sciences are recognized by the corresponding ministerial authorities. Official recognition by a branch of the government, but not the Ministry of Education, may be acceptable. In some countries, private postsecondary education is not recognized, in others the recognition of postsecondary private institutions/programs is approved by a separate entity within the country, such as CONESUP (*Consejo de Educación Superior Privada*–Higher Private Education Council) in Latin America. The Web site www.conesup. net lists private institutions/programs recognized in Latin America.

Currently, many countries are expanding their quality assurance efforts in education and the list of approved or closed institutions from Russia to Southern Africa changes constantly. In El Salvador, the award of law degrees to unqualified individuals that had not completed programs became a national scandal a few years ago and lead to the suspension of judges who were practicing with fraudulent "titulos." The *Conseil Africain et Malgache pour l'Enseignement Supérieur* (CAMES) is currently discussing the impact the increasing frequency of fraud is having on the general acceptability of African degrees in the world (Nigeria and the Democratic Republic of Congo cited). Seventeen nations are participating. These are Benin, Burkina Faso, Burundi, Cameroon, Central Africa Republic, Congo, Côte d'Ivoire, Gabon, Guinea, Madagascar, Mali, Niger, Rwanda, Democratic Republic of Congo, Senegal, Chad and Togo.

When program accreditation (*e.g.*, acupuncture, engineering, medicine) is sought, the analyst needs to be aware that program approval may fall under the purview of the corresponding professional field. For information on engineering program recognition in several countries, such as Australia, Hong Kong, South Africa, or the UK, analysts may want to visit the Institution of Engineers Australia (www.ieaust.org.au), the Hong Kong Institution of Engineers (www.hkie.org.hk), The Engineering Council of South Africa, (www.ecsa.co.za), the Engineering Council, UK (www.engc.org.uk), or the *Commission de Titres d'Ingénieurs* in France, (www.commission-cti.fr/site_flash/fr/index_flash.htm).

The issue of official recognition gets more complicated when schools claim to be affiliated to an institution in the U.S. or any other country. The words chartered, affiliated, operating in cooperation with, internationally accredited or recognized and the term *"authorisation provisoire de fonctionnement"* (temporary license to function), used recently to described the current status of the Autonomous University of Port-au-Prince in Haiti, may be a clue. This should alert a credential analyst to investigate the legal recognition of any postsecondary institution claiming to be accredited or awarding "accredited degrees." The claim that an institution is accredited or recognized by an international accreditation agency should also raise questions because accreditation is a national process not a global operation. This issue should be of particular interest to professionals in the study abroad profession because of the program affiliations and exchange agreements constantly sought between higher education institutions. Consultation with national educational authorities should precede any serious considerations for collaborative agreements.

For information on U.S. accreditation, visit www.chea.org. The Council on Higher Education Accreditation (CHEA) also publishes an annual list of accredited U.S. institutions located both in the U.S. and abroad. It is advisable to check schools with Americanized names and/or U.S. addresses against that list, *e.g.*, "American University of Hawaii-India." A list of regional, national and program accreditors is included in the CHEA publication.

The publication *Degree Mills, The Billion Dollar Industry that has Sold More than a Million Fake Diplomas* by John Bear and Allen Ezell (2005), is a guide to this industry and its products, and includes a list of more than 200 unrecognized accreditors. For additional information on this topic, analysts may want to visit the Oregon Office of Degree Authorization web site, www.osac.state.or.us/oda/ and a site prepared by Professor G. Gollin, University of Illinois at Urbana-Champaign, www.hep.uiuc.edu/home/g-gollin/.

If you are unable to find a satisfactory answer to the four questions listed above, then your doubts may be more than just a hunch. The quasi-scientific analysis of questionable credentials has three major facets:

- ◆ Clue Identification
- ◆ Analysis and Investigation
- ◆ Verification of facts

Where is the clue?

The feeling that something is wrong or just a simple hunch is, for the seasoned credential analyst, the beginning of a journey that may lead to an irrevocable truth: you are dealing with some form of fraud. Regardless of your experience in credential analysis, the road to establish the legitimacy of a document begins with the obvious: checking each vital component of the document in question to determine if any of the signs listed below are present.

- ◆ Discrepancies/inconsistencies noted in the application for admission
- ◆ Evidence of corrected personal data (name, birth date, gender)
- ◆ Evidence of white-out, burn-marks, erasures, corrections
- ◆ Interrupted/obliterated lines where information is generally typed or printed
- ◆ Missing pictures in diplomas or professional identification cards

- Partial seals on the surface of superimposed pictures not on the document surface
- Incompatible type-face in a single document
- Irregular spacing between words or letters, or insufficient space for the text
- Unprofessional language, poor grammar, misspellings
- Questionable paper quality, texture, size (letter or legal), coloration
- Ink color and quality
- Incorrect seals/emblems, colors, shapes
- Inappropriate or outdated signatures
- Signature aberrations including shading and continuity
- Cultural and anachronistic inconsistencies (dates, institutional name changes, institutional mergers, institutional closures)
- Educational aberrations (hours of study, uncharacteristic grading system, years of study, program cancellations)
- Non-traditional format of transcripts or grade certificates prepared in a language other than the official language of the country where the document originated. Always bear in mind that many countries are currently issuing official transcripts in English: Japan, Korea, Taiwan, Philippines, Thailand, Canada (except Quebec), Kuwait, Saudi Arabia, Iraq, Egypt, Israel, Oman, Bahrain, and the United Arab Emirates.
- Numerical aberrations: credits do not add up and overall grade point averages are a mathematical impossibility
- Creative translations showing American grades, American courses titles, an uncharacteristic or exorbitant number of credit or hours per class
- Presence of various unusually high grades in countries where higher grade ranges are virtually nonexistent

During the initial review process, it is important to keep in mind that, although secondary examination certificates (*e.g.*, School Leaving Certificates), transcripts and grade certificates in many countries are preprinted, documents in some parts of the world are still manually prepared using a typewriter or word processor. Also, grades are normally hand written in an examination score card or leaving certificate. However, the document format, the preprinted information revealing the authority officiating the examinations and endorsing or approving the conferral of the award, the corresponding signatures and the customary seals are constant and should be reviewed as part of your initial inspection. In many countries, the only official secondary school certificate is given to the student. Familiarity with the appearance and genetic characteristics of the document, among other things might help identify initially if a certificate is official.

Analysis and Investigation—General Methodology

- Know the educational system you are working with.
- Compare biographical data (date of birth, name, sex) on all documents to make sure everything belongs to the person whose application you are reviewing.
- Review the self-reported educational data with the documents received to determine whether anything is missing. Request any missing information or documentation using the academic terminology used in the country. If you use your own terminology (*e.g.*, transcript) you may get a manufactured document.
- Question any 'gaps' in the educational history.
- Verify whether the institution exists, and if it existed at the time of the award.
- Verify if the student has gone through a name change and that this is properly reflected in the official documentation.
- Find out what body recognizes the institution. Is it from an entity you will accept?
- Check if the program (major/degree) is offered, if it existed at the time it was issued.
- Find out if the duration (three to four years, etc.) or structure (annual, semester, etc.) of the program has changed. This information can be found these days on institutional web sites.
- Confirm that the degree was awarded. In many countries, a transcript or certificate states program completion but there is no reference to degree awarded. Since the award is contingent upon satisfactory completion of comprehensive examinations, a research or graduation project, and in some instances a period of community work or practical training, the official proof of degree earned must be requested to confirm degree

earned. If a degree is claimed, then the evidence is available and universities can confirm it.

- Make sure that the document you are reviewing conforms to previously reviewed documents from the same country, in the same time period, and reflects what your resources indicate they would look like.

- Verify if the degree is issued in one language or is a bilingual document. For instance, degrees from some African countries may be issued in French and Arabic, or in French and Somali (*e.g.*, Mauritania, Morocco, Somalia).

- Review all correspondence received and where it was postmarked. In the case of express courier, track the package shipments. The suspicion that academic documents from Somalia were fraudulent a few years ago was confirmed when the express mail package apparently originating in Somalia was from a carrier that had suspended its service to this country.

- Be cautious of applications submitted just before deadlines, making verification almost impossible. As the saying goes, "Someone else's lack of planning does not constitute your emergency."

Verification Check List

- If your initial review and suspicion starts with a photocopy, request the original; modern copy machines can produce perfect photocopies that obliterate any vestiges of alterations.

- Write to the issuing institution/awarding authority, including a copy of the document in question, but never the suspected 'original'.

- Determine who is the appropriate university authority to receive and act on your inquiry (the role of preparing official documents varies and so does the title of the individual [*e.g.*, Controller of Examinations in India]). If original inquiries fail, send the letter to the President, Rector or General Secretary. Overseas advisers are extremely helpful because they can provide valuable information about the educational system and its recognized institutions; most importantly, they can provide you with the address, phone/fax numbers, and e-mail of the appropriate officials.

- Introduce your institution/organization and state the reason for the evaluation and needed verification.

- Outline clearly your observations and ask specific questions about the information you need clarified.
- If your document contains color or embossed seals describe them and ask for confirmation that what you received matches the traditional institutional features.
- Be clear about what information you want to verify (*e.g.*, dates of attendance, accuracy of grades, contact/credit hours, course listings), or received (*e.g.*, confirmation of degree earned).
- Include your contact information and a 'case reference code' to be included in the response.
- Indicate the date you wish to receive a response and include your mailing address, fax number and e-mail information. In a few cases, institutions have contacted me to request additional data so that they may conduct investigations to determine if the document was manufactured internally.
- Keep a copy of the verification letter in a separate file in case the response has no 'reference code.'
- Review your verification file on a regular basis and send a second verification request to an alternate institutional official indicating the date the previous inquiry was sent.
- If you find possible discrepancies, inconsistencies, etc., and/or are unsure about the authenticity of a document, ask a colleague for a second opinion or recommendations on useful tools to proceed with your initial assessment.

When the Outcome is Fraud

In order to effectively handle the resolution of a fraud investigation it is important to:

- Keep a record of your investigation including a descriptive account of the questionable facts, listing your observations and documenting your findings.
- Obtain official verification in writing specifying the type of fraud committed and keep the envelope in which it arrived. For legal purposes, you should ask for an original response even if the quick response

arrives via fax or electronic mail. The latter may not be acceptable in a court of law and the origin or the response may be questionable.

◆ When notifying individuals of your findings, include the same "terminology" used by the institution/officials sending the verification.

◆ Develop a system to track and identify fraudulent applicants, they have a way of turning up unexpectedly like a bad penny with new records, new stories, and new tricks.

When you are dealing with individuals already on campus:

◆ Keep a record of your investigation as described above. This is vital in the event you are challenged and legal counsel intervenes.

◆ Take appropriate action against the offender. From an academic/institutional perspective, you must review and or define your policies and procedures and enforce the penalties. They should not be any different than those used for domestic students.

Helpful Procedures to Prevent Fraud

We cannot stop fraud from happening but we can create the structure and mechanism to guard against it by establishing measures to control and minimize its occurrence:

◆ Accept only official transcripts whenever possible and degree verification sent directly by the issuing institution in a sealed envelope and post marked in the foreign country; keep envelopes and stamps. When only one original is issued, a certified or attested copy by the record keeping authorities in the institution may be used.

◆ Be aware of scanned color copies; they look real but removable components such as pictures and legalization stamps are not detachable.

◆ Do not expect notarized copies to be a guarantee of legitimacy or accuracy. The notary does not verify the content and validity of a document, only the authenticity of the signature.

◆ Accept only official *literal* translations that *mirror* the content of the document in the original language. Often times, interpretative translations include the conversion of grades from a numerical to a letter grade, and 80 on a Chinese document is translated as "A."

- Translations should be done and authenticated by the appropriate authorities in the home country.
- Never use English translations in lieu of original language documents to evaluate and make admissions determinations. Translations should be used as a "road map" to identify and confirm critical information. Remember, for every translation there is an original.
- Generally, there should be no similarity between the fonts used in the original and the translated document if separate sources (the institution and the translator) prepared them.
- Learn to identify key terminology/symbols/characters in the native language document to confirm the accuracy of a translation. Learn the numerical symbols in Arabic, Farsi and Chinese languages to verify numerical accuracy. Identify useful resources (dictionaries, colleagues, faculty, etc.)
- Be aware of which countries issue documents in English. Currently, these countries include Japan, Korea, Taiwan, Philippines, Thailand, Canada (except Quebec), Kuwait, Saudi Arabia, Iraq, Egypt, Israel, Oman, Bahrain, and the United Arab Emirates. Do not forget that in some countries diplomas are issued in two languages (national and official), *e.g.*, some African nations and former Soviet Republics.
- Develop a customized credential bank to facilitate in-house credential verification.
- Bookmark useful educational Web sites that might help you in your research for the truth.

The task of analyzing the legitimacy of academic credentials demands constant awareness of educational changes and world affairs, the ability to network and expand our spheres of operation, and the sharpness of a trained eye to see beyond appearances. Although one should not always operate under the assumption than everyone is guilty of fraud until proven innocent, the reality is that one should recognize as well as question when the picture is not right.

I could have never written this article or pursued my passion for credential fraud detection had it not been for the teaching, mentoring and encouragement received from various colleagues in the field who were always willing to share their findings, experience and wisdom, and who continue to zealously guard the credibility and ethics of our profession. Let's keep fighting for those who make their education an honest learning experience, not a trip to "Diploma Ville."

BIBLIOGRAPHY

Adan, Eva-Angela, J. Bell, and N. Katz. 2004. The Naked Truth behind Fraudulent Academic Credentials. NAFSA Annual Conference Workshop.

de Leew, Herman. 2002. *On the Authenticity of Educational Credentials from the Kurdish Autonomous Zone in Northern Iraq.* Informatie Beheer Groep: Netherlands.

de Leeuw, Herman. 2006. Dealing with document fraud—The case of Afghanistan. *ADSEC Newsletter.* August 25.

Koenig, Ann M. and E. Devlin. 2004. International Diploma Mills and Bogus Credentials. Presentation at the Western States Certification Conference, June 2004.

Hilton, Ordway. 1993. *Scientific Examination of Questioned Documents.* CRC Press LLC: FL.

(No Author). 2004. Les universitaires togolais cherchent à revaloriser les diplômes. *République Togolaise.* July 20. Available at: <www.republicoftogo.com/fr/news/news.asp?rubID=1&srubID=65&themeID=1&newsID=8334>.

The Columbia Electronic Encyclopedia, 6th ed. s.v. "fraud." Retrieved 23 November 2004 from <http://aol1.infoplease.com/ce6/society/A0819522.html>.

✗✗✗✗✗✗✗✗✗✗✗✗✗✗✗✗✗✗✗

CHAPTER THREE

A Practical Guide to Documentation Review and Verification in International Admissions

by Ann M. Koenig and Jane Yahr Shepard

There are many reasons why an applicant with foreign educational records would submit fraudulent or misleading documents to a college or university in the United States. These range from a sincere desire to be admitted to the institution, to an attempt to obtain an institution's official admissions documentation so that it can be altered and sold for a variety of illegal purposes. We as international admissions officers and credential evaluators must be alert to the reality that applicants do submit spurious documents. Our best protection against our institutions becoming victims of foreign educational record fraud is a solid knowledge base among our foreign document evaluators, and a strong network of information sharing about verification successes.

Best practice in the international admissions office calls for:

◆ training and continuing professional development for foreign record evaluators so that they are knowledgeable and up-to-date about country educational systems, documentation practices, and events that impact international education;

◆ clear communication to applicants about the documentation required for admission;

- careful review of the documents that are submitted;
- requests for verification of suspicious documents;
- appropriate follow-up when verification is received from the issuing institution or educational authority;
- and sharing success stories in the verification process.

This article is based on a presentation given by the authors that outlined step-by-step guidelines for admissions professionals and foreign document evaluators to implement these principles of best practice. The session also included an interactive review of a variety of spurious documents actually submitted by applicants to U.S. institutions that illustrated the concepts outlined in the guidelines. Discussion among the session participants focused on institutional policies on documentation, resources for evaluation and verification, and approaches to handling cases in which the documentation submitted was confirmed as being fraudulent.

Goal 1: To Assemble a Complete File of Authentic Records

The first goal in working with an application for admission is to assemble a complete file of authentic documents that provide all of the information needed to do an accurate evaluation.

◆ Learning about Documentation Practices: The Importance of Resources and Networking

Evaluators need to consult reliable resources on country educational systems and documentation practices, and learn to identify what constitutes official and authentic documentation. It is very important for evaluators to stay abreast of country information and current events that impact on issues in international admissions—by attending professional conferences and workshops, using print and electronic sources of information and current awareness services, and networking with colleagues. The knowledge base, skills, and experience required to work with international applicants and foreign educational records effectively can only be gained and honed by an investment in reliable resources and continuing professional development.

24 | *Guide to Bogus Institutions and Documents*
A Practical Guide to Documentation Review and
Verification in International Admissions

◆ Use of English Translations

In order to do an accurate assessment of applicants' previous education, evaluators should insist on receiving official documents in the original language in which they are issued. English translations may be needed, and evaluators need to establish guidelines on how English translations will be used in the evaluation process. Evaluations should never be based on translations alone.

English translations should be literal, complete, word-for-word representations of the language in the original documents, prepared in the same format as the original, by a person familiar with both languages. If the evaluator is not familiar with foreign languages, a professional English translation may be required. However, evaluators should keep in mind that the most important facet of translation is accuracy in representing exactly what is written in the foreign language. The issue of *who* does the translation is secondary to the question of *how accurate* it is. In some cases, a student, friend of the applicant, or faculty member may be able to provide an English translation that is as accurate as a translation done by a professional translator.

The accuracy of the translation should be confirmed by the use of reliable resources on the educational system of the country that uses the indigenous terminology. The evaluator should base the evaluation on the original document, using the English translation only as a tool.

If the translation appears to be inaccurate or misleading, then the applicant should be required to submit a different, accurate translation. There is no reason why an evaluator should hesitate in requesting an accurate English translation if one is needed. Likewise, evaluators should not jump to conclusions about the authenticity of the original document, or the applicant's intentions, if the English translation is not accurate. The translation is a tool for understanding the official document; any judgments about the authenticity of an official document should be based on the document itself, not on the English translation.

◆ Communicating with Applicants About Documentation Requirements

The key to actually receiving appropriate documentation from applicants is to tell them what documentation is required. A *proactive* admissions

Guide to Bogus Institutions and Documents
A Practical Guide to Documentation Review and
Verification in International Admissions   25

office steers its applicants toward submitting a complete application file, rather than *reacting* to whatever documentation the student submits. Information on documentation requirements should be shared with the prospect or applicant the very first time they contact the admissions office, because, as experienced international admissions officers know, obtaining official academic documents from foreign countries can be a lengthy and frustrating process.

Wording about documentation requirements, whether shared verbally, in print, or electronically, should be very precise and clear, and include the indigenous terminology for the documents required. Using the native terms for the name of the credential, the type of institution, and the office of the institution that issues official documents, for example, can help a student understand exactly what type of documentation is required. It can also help to avoid the all-too-common situation in which the u.s. institution finally receives "the document," only to discover that the document received isn't the official one that the u.s. institution requires.

◆ Establishing a Reference Collection

Effective evaluators develop a resource collection that includes copies of authentic documents they have received, reliable resources on country and documentation information, and a network of trusted colleagues who can help them stay informed about foreign educational systems and current events. Easy access to good resources is essential to learning to make good professional judgments if applicants say they cannot get required documentation, or if the documentation really is not available. Floods, volcanic eruptions, hurricanes, war, and other such catastrophic events have indeed destroyed student records in educational institutions within the last ten years, even in the United States, but such occurrences are rare, and they usually can be confirmed by reliable sources. When students claim that their diplomas or academic certificates have been destroyed or otherwise lost, it is important to know how to verify that information and then obtain alternative documentation of the student's educational background.

26 | *Guide to Bogus Institutions and Documents*
A Practical Guide to Documentation Review and
Verification in International Admissions

◆ **Communicating About the Consequences of Submitted Falsified Documentation**

In addition to outlining the required documents for admission, the admissions office should define clearly what happens if incomplete, untrue, or falsified information or documentation is submitted. If an applicant's file is incomplete, how is the applicant informed of what is still missing from the file? If there are gaps in the student's self-reported educational history, or self-reported data do not match the information indicated on official records, what is the follow-up procedure? The admissions office needs to determine appropriate courses of action for such cases, based on the professional judgment of evaluators, and convey this information to applicants up front.

◆ **Action Plan**

▶ Identify opportunities to learn more about country educational systems, documentation issuing practices in other countries, and significant events abroad that impact on education and student mobility.

Tips: Use training programs, publications and Web-based resources offered by AACRAO, NAFSA, credential evaluation services; have direct interaction with students and faculty from other countries; visit current awareness services (electronic discussion lists, news Web sites). AACRAO's International Education Services (www.aacrao.org/international/foreignEdCred.cfm) is a good starting point.

▶ Based on accurate information from informed and reliable sources, develop guidelines or policies on the documents required to complete a file, the time frames for applicants to submit acceptable documentation, how applicants are informed about what they must submit, and what happens if they submit incomplete or unacceptable documentation. Adjust guidelines and requirements as appropriate and according to your office's experiences.

▶ Identify and implement ways to inform applicants about documentation requirements the first time you have contact with them.

Guide to Bogus Institutions and Documents
A Practical Guide to Documentation Review and
Verification in International Admissions

27

> ► Determine the parameters of negotiability (if any) on acceptable documentation, and act judiciously within those parameters, in a manner that creates a positive situation for all sides, if possible.

Goal 2: To Establish the Authenticity of the Documentation Submitted

Most admissions offices are swamped with work, from recruiting prospects to responding to inquiries to reviewing applications to communicating admissions decisions to running orientation programs. In this atmosphere, it is sometimes difficult to take the time needed to review documentation carefully with an eye for authenticity of documentation. Establishing a standard step-by-step approach to document review can help evaluators to be thorough yet efficient.

◆ **Suggested Step-by-Step Approach to Documentation Review:**
> ► Determine whether the documents are acceptable according to the guidelines you have established.
> ► Arrange the documents in chronological order. Review the biographical data and educational history provided by the applicant and compare with the "story" told by the documents. Pay attention to detail (location, age, level of education, quality of performance, test results, military service, employment history, etc.).
> ► Use reliable resources to confirm the status, type, and level of the institution or authority that issued each document.
> ► Confirm that the format of each document is consistent with that of other documents from the same institution or authority, from the same era. Refer to your sample document file and standard resources.
> ► Confirm the content of each document. Actually *read it*.
>> ▷ Double-check the biographical information.
>> ▷ Look for key words that give you vital information.
>> ▷ Identify the dates of attendance.
>> ▷ Review the content of the program or courses represented. Do the courses listed correspond to the field of study in which the student was enrolled?

28 | *Guide to Bogus Institutions and Documents*
A Practical Guide to Documentation Review and
Verification in International Admissions

▷ Determine whether courses or programs were completed, and compare the assessment results (grades, marks, %, etc.) with information on the country's/institution's grading scale.

▷ Is there any information missing from the document that should be there?

▷ Is there information on the document that shouldn't be there?

▷ Are words spelled correctly in the native language?

▷ If the document is in a language that you don't understand, use key terms and phrases in the native language along with a dictionary and reliable evaluation resources to confirm the accuracy of the English translation. (Never work solely from an English translation if the document was issued in a language other than English; see above.) Check the translations of other documents from the same country or institution if you are unsure about the translation, or request that a new translation be done by a different translator. Keep a list of reliable translators handy.

▶ If you find discrepancies, problems, omissions, inconsistencies, etc., have "another set of eyes" review the document and your resource materials with you. Ask colleagues who are knowledgeable about the particular country, institution, or field of study to review the document with you.

▶ If the problem cannot be resolved by checking resources and with input from colleagues...

▶ **Get verification.** (See Chapter One, "Why Verification of Suspicious Foreign Records is Important," on page 1.)

Goal 3: To Obtain Verification of Suspicious Documents

◆ **Preparing a Request for Verification**

In preparing to send a verification request, the evaluator must identify the office or person to whom the verification request should be sent, locate the appropriate contact information for this office or person, and consider the most effective way to send the verification request (postal service, courier service, fax, e-mail, telephone, etc.). A reliable resource network,

Guide to Bogus Institutions and Documents
A Practical Guide to Documentation Review and
Verification in International Admissions | 29

made up of publications and newsletters, electronic resources, and trusted colleagues, can be very helpful in identifying this information.

Next, the evaluator needs to formulate the request for verification. It is helpful to develop a standard form or letter to request verification, so as not to have to "reinvent the wheel" each time verification is needed.

Some suggestions for preparing a verification request:

- Determine whether the request should be written in English or another language, or both, to get a response as soon as possible. If in a language other than English, prepare the request in English first and have it translated by a reliable translator, such as a faculty or staff member. Send the request both in English and the other language.
- Clearly state "Request for Verification" in the opening of the request letter.
- Introduce yourself, your institution and the reason you are requesting verification (student has applied for admission at your institution; student has requested transfer credit based on these documents; etc.).
- Outline your observations about the inconsistencies in the document. Include a copy of it, with problem areas highlighted.
- Be clear and specific about what information you need to receive from the verifier. For example, if the document is not authentic, what further information would you want to know?
- Specify a date by which you need a response, if you have a specific time frame, the format in which a response would be acceptable (for example, must be in writing), and the language in which you need to receive the response.
- Include your contact information for the response.
- Include a reference code (identifying information for you) and ask the verifier to include it in the response.
- Request confidentiality. This information is not to be shared with the student or anyone else.
- Thank the reader and offer to assist in the future or send a catalog or other informational material from your institution.

30 | *Guide to Bogus Institutions and Documents*
A Practical Guide to Documentation Review and
Verification in International Admissions

▶ Once you have sent the verification request, place a copy of it in the applicant's file. Also start a "Verification Requests" file where you keep copies of request letters and the documents until you receive a response. Cross-reference the files so that you can easily retrieve the applicant's file when the response is received.

◆ Communicating with Colleagues About Requests for Verification

Every admissions officer must also deal with the question of how and what to communicate to the student or applicant about the verification process. This judgment usually involves a certain amount of speculation about how, why, when and where an applicant may have altered documents or obtained falsified documents and about why suspicious documents were submitted with the application. In our role as "document detectives," speculations about intention and mode of operation can act as a "sixth sense" in leading us in certain directions to get the information we need to "crack the case." But until the documents have been reviewed by the issuing authority and verified as either legitimate or spurious, the evaluator's speculations or suspicions should be kept private and should be shared only with colleagues or supervisors who can help determine how to proceed to obtain official verification from the issuing authority.

◆ Communicating with Applicants About Requests for Verification

Strategies for communicating with students or applicants can range from saying nothing at all to the applicant to informing the applicant that the evaluator has concerns about the documents and asking for explanations and/or assistance in getting verification or "better" documents to informing the applicant that verification has been requested and that nothing further will be done until verification has been received. Each case involving suspicious documentation needs to be reviewed on an individual basis and handled with a sensitivity to the circumstances of the particular case. Again, working with trusted resources, including experienced colleagues who have successfully navigated cases like these, helps admissions officers and evaluators to develop good professional judgment about how to handle cases involving suspicious documents.

Guide to Bogus Institutions and Documents
A Practical Guide to Documentation Review and | 31
Verification in International Admissions

Goal 4: To Complete the Verification Process and Follow Up as Appropriate

The receipt of a verification letter is one of the most thrilling experiences in the international admissions office. There are many countries from which it is difficult to get verification, due to factors that we in the United States higher education community may take for granted—limited financial, human and technological resources; differences in recordkeeping systems; corruption; disruptions in civil life because of natural disasters or warfare. Despite the best intentions of our colleagues abroad, we cannot always count on their cooperation in a procedure that is part of the standard of professional practice in educational administration in the United States. Thus receiving a response to a verification request is the first step in the resolution of a tense and difficult situation involving the institution and the student.

◆ **Assessing the Response**

Once the verification is received, the evaluator needs to assess the response and determine a further course of action, if needed:

▸ Does the information provided adequately answer the evaluator's concerns about the authenticity of the document? Is it conclusive?

▸ If the documents are verified as being spurious, how will the admissions office follow up with the student? Procedures for handling this situation, and guidelines for the consequences to applicants who submit falsified documents, should be defined and communicated to staff and applicants well before this stage of the admissions review process. Now that the documents have been verified as fraudulent, how does the evaluator follow up with the student?

▸ If the information provided is not conclusive, what further action needs to be taken? Will another round of correspondence be fruitful? To whom should it be addressed? What other avenues can be pursued if it seems that further contact with the verifying authority would not be productive?

▸ What if the verifying authority requests further information or documentation from the evaluator? There might be a request for the student's current contact information, for example, so that the authority

Guide to Bogus Institutions and Documents
A Practical Guide to Documentation Review and
Verification in International Admissions

can contact the student directly regarding questionable or fraudulent documents. What is the receiving institution's responsibility in responding to such a request?

▶ What if a verification fee is requested? Some educational authorities have begun assessing a fee for verification, particularly in areas where resources are limited, or a large number of verification requests are received. How does the evaluator handle such a situation?

◆ Acting on Conclusive Verification that Documentation is Fraudulent

When conclusive, authoritative verification of fraudulent documentation has been received, the institution needs to follow up with the applicant or student according to the guidelines established for such cases. Policies and procedures should already be in place, so that a standard protocol is followed. Each case involving fraudulent documents has different circumstances, and as new twists and perspectives come to light, strategies for dealing with them can be incorporated into the institutional response to this scenario.

◆ Another Valuable Resource for the Reference Collection

Every request for verification and response received represents valuable material for the evaluator's resource collection. The "Verification Request" file should be updated with each response received. Evaluators should note who actually verified the documentation, contact information for that person or office, how long the process took, and any other information that could be useful for future verification requests. Archiving each successive case in which documents needed to be verified makes the next case easier.

◆ Sharing Verification Success and Information with the International Education Community

Evaluators and admissions officers need to share news of their verification successes with the international education community. Word needs to "get around" whenever we receive authoritative, conclusive confirmation of fraudulent foreign documents. Electronic discussion lists, professional

Guide to Bogus Institutions and Documents
A Practical Guide to Documentation Review and | 33
Verification in International Admissions

development venues, telephone conversations with colleagues—all are appropriate arenas for us to share our verification successes.

Resources For Information/Verification

◆ Your very own "Resources" collection
◆ Printed resources
  ▶ Printed materials from institutions and education authorities
  ▶ Directories of universities worldwide
  ▶ Country-/region-specific publications from AACRAO, PIER, NAFSA, private organizations
  ▶ general overviews of country educational systems
  ▶ evaluation guides published by colleagues in other countries
  ▶ Check the AACRAO Publications Catalog for useful resources in print (www.aacrao.org/publications/catalog.cfm)
  ▶ The NAFSA ADSEC Bibliography contains bibliographic and ordering information for many publication. Go to www.nafsa.org and search "International Admissions Bibliography."

◆ Electronic resources
  ▶ AACRAO's International Education Services (www.aacrao.org/international/foreignEdCred.cfm) offers publications, training opportunities, foreign credential evaluation services, consulting services, and more.
  ▶ The NAFSA ADSEC home page provides links to many excellent online resources (www.adsec.nafsa.org/).
  ▶ The European Association for International Education ACE (Admissions Officers' and Credential Evaluators') Web pages at www.eaie.org/ACE/ and www.aic.lv/ace/ are useful tools, including links to other resources.

◆ Electronic discussion lists and networking tools such as Inter-L (go to http://groups.yahoo.com/ and Search "Inter-L")
◆ U.S. Department of State Advising Centers (http://educationusa.state.gov/centers/) can assist you with specific questions about education in a particular country.

- Overseas advisors have contacts throughout their geographic regions who can help you. Go to www.nafsa.org and search "Overseas Educational Advising Network."
- Country experts, authors of country and regional resource works, conference session presenters, workshop leaders, etc. may have detailed information in their research files.
- Consulates/embassies in the United States. They may have contact information for institutions and/or education authorities.
- Your campus or institutional contacts within the country. Your institution may already have contacts with colleagues in the country who can help you find out where to get assistance and information.

Guide to Bogus Institutions and Documents
A Practical Guide to Documentation Review and | 35
Verification in International Admissions

⬦⬦⬦⬦⬦⬦⬦⬦⬦⬦⬦⬦⬦⬦⬦

CHAPTER FOUR

Transcript Fraud and Handling Fraudulent Documents

by Alan Ezell

Transcript fraud is a common problem for colleges and universities, businesses, employers, governmental licensing boards, and other agencies, with some experiencing it more so than others. The only difference between a large and small institution is the volume of degree and transcript fraud it experiences.

What is transcript fraud?

Transcript fraud can be defined as:

⬦ any alteration to a legitimately issued transcript from a genuine college or university, by which the student's name, Social Security or student identification number, age, courses, grades, grade point average (GPA), graduation status, or any other information on the document, is changed or deleted, or information that does not belong to the original document is added;

⬦ any creation of a document purporting to be a transcript issued by a fictional college or university (so-called "diploma mill" or "degree mill"); or

⬦ any creation of a document purporting to be an official record of academic work, showing courses or other academic work, with grades and/

or credit, in which the student did not actually enroll, did not complete, for which appropriate academic work was not required, or which otherwise does not reflect real and/or appropriate academic achievement.

Transcript fraud is an international problem. Never once think that degree mills and transcript fraud exist only in the United States; fraudulent transcripts are routinely received by colleges, universities, employers, and government offices on a worldwide basis.

What are the types of fraudulent transcripts?

Generally, fraudulent transcripts fall into the following major categories:

◆ Transcripts issued by legitimate accredited institutions which are later altered.

◆ Transcripts from fictional/fraudulent/unaccredited institutions.

◆ Counterfeit transcripts produced with the names of legitimate accredited institutions, either based on real transcripts or on fabrications meant to look like real ones.

Why do we have transcript fraud?

Transcript fraud exists today in order to:

◆ Show academic degree(s) not earned

◆ Report as completed a major, or area of concentration, for which some requirements were not satisfied, or which the student never actually took

◆ Falsify reference to age

◆ Qualify for financial aid by altering dates of attendance

◆ Show coursework not taken

◆ Alter grades in hopes of enhancing employability

◆ Change the name of the record holder

◆ Change the name of the record holder as part of an identity assumption. Identity fraud is the fastest growing form of white-collar crime today.

How does transcript fraud come to light?

Transcript Fraud normally comes to light when your institution receives inquiries resulting from:

- Pre-employment background checks
- Employee performing poorly on the job
- Individual applying for advanced degree or specialized training program, or
- Other requests for verification of degree as based on unusual circumstances.

It can be as simple as a candidate for a local school board calling to verify the degree and transcript of his opponent. Or it may be a professor calling while writing a letter of recommendation for a valued colleague, and learning that his fellow worker has never completed his degree.

Once a person places false educational claims in his or her resume, job application, or on a Web site, it is analogous to placing a lit stick of dynamite in the resume. The question is not if it will explode, but when.

For example, an individual forged several transcripts from a well-known Midwestern university, whereby he claimed undergraduate and graduate degrees in Engineering. He then falsified a Ph.D. degree in Engineering from an unrelated institution, and formed a medical consulting business in Florida with a well-known physician. When this medical consulting business could not produce results commensurate with their alleged training, a client called the named issuing institutions to verify the degrees. The ensuing lawsuit resulted in a judgment for the plaintiff in the amount of $327,271.48.

What is available on the Internet today?

Simply put: anything and everything is found on the Internet. You (and your students, former students, and members of the general public), can, with a click of the mouse (and a credit card), purchase any of the following with no impunity:

- Degree and transcript in the name of your institution (on security paper, with hologram and other security features)
- Envelopes bearing return address, logo (if any) of your institution
- Registrar's Office rubber stamps, metal seal, etc.
- A toll-free telephone number for degree verification, or
- A third party transcript records archive service with accompanying degree verification.

Some of today's Web sites offer to sell actual degree and transcript replicas, whereas others will sell you a template from which you can print the degree and transcript yourself. Most of these Web sites attempt to limit their liability with disclaimers indicating that the degrees and transcripts are being sold for "entertainment purposes only" or as "novelty items."

In order to protect yourself and your institution, examine the following Web sites to see if/where your school's name appears. Keep in mind that this list represents a sampling; there are many more Web sites like those shown in Table 1. (Also, see Figure 1 on page 43.)

Are degrees and transcripts (on security paper) in the name of your institution for sale on the Web sites below? What have you done about this? If your institution does not attempt to put a halt to this, then why should law enforcement, since it is your good name that is at stake?

Table 1. Example Diploma Mill Web sites		
Web site	Number of Institutions Whose Diplomas Are...	
	For Sale	Not Offered
instantdegrees.com	Unknown	Unknown
diplomasforless.com	261	16+ states of CT and IL
phonydiplomas.com	Unknown	Unknown
customdegrees.com	Unknown	Unknown
genuinedegrees.com	Unknown	Unknown
diplomaville.com	350+	0
diplomaservices.com	173	24
fantasydiplomas.com	254	21
affordabledegrees.com	1	0
righttrackref.com	3,500	0

What can you do? Be proactive.

Your objective is to move your school's name from the "Schools Offered" list to the "Schools Not Offered" list. Although we might laugh at the names of these Web sites, the number of such sites is growing steadily, indicating an increasing demand for their products. In turn, this is causing your office to receive an increased number of calls for verification of fraudulent credentials that bear the name and seals/stamps of your institution.

BROKERS, YOUR SECURITY PAPER, AND FRAUDULENT OUTSOURCED SERVICES

Several of the fraudsters who sell replicas of your degrees and transcripts are quite enterprising. While some have established "brokers," some offer flat "commissions" on sales, and others have established "affiliate" networks, selling links of their Web sites to others, thus receiving first (15 percent), second (5 percent), and third (2 percent) level commissions for degree and transcript sales. Also, in order to increase sales, some also offer a "free verification service" depending on the institutional document they are selling.

You and your institution should also be alert for those fraudsters who are not only selling replicas of your degrees and transcripts, but are also selling various rubber stamps, envelopes, seals, and security paper, all in your name. When this is detected, identify the persons offering these items for sale, then take action.

Just as some colleges and universities have outsourced some of the functions of the registrar's office to outside companies, the fraudsters have created their own entities in order to "blend in." We have seen an increased number of purported independent third party transcript archive and verification centers, which provide toll-free telephone numbers where a caller can obtain "graduate verification." Generally, these entities are also operated by the same fraudsters who produced the fictitious documents.

Many use a Washington, D.C. address as part of their camouflage of legitimacy. Of course, this is done to add an air of authenticity to the dubious supporting documents, such as transcripts from the notorious St. Regis University, purportedly a Liberian university. AACRAO's International Education Services office has a St. Regis University transcript on file that shows a toll-free 877 telephone number for "Saint Regis Verifications," as well as the address and telephone number of the Official Transcript Archive Center (OTAC) (www.transcriptarchive.com), formerly of 611 Pennsylvania Avenue, S.E., Washington, D.C., now at 1812 Marsh Road, Suite 6-242, Wilmington, Delaware.

Another example using a Washington, D.C. address to give the impression of legitimacy is the National Academic Archive Registrar (www.academic-archive.com), 4401 Connecticut Avenue, N.W. LBBY A #121, Washington, D.C., which is, not surprisingly, the address of a UPS commercial mail facility.

These purported archivists use mail drop addresses in Washington, D.C. in an effort to appear official, national in scope, or associated with the United States government. Their Web sites state that they verify no documents given to them; they just act as a "clearinghouse" for both institutions and individuals. Their fees charged give a new meaning to the words "à la carte," as can be seen when you examine their fee schedule.

Ironically, when viewing the OTAC Web site above, you will note links to "Apostille Services" and "Degree Evaluation Attestation." Both of these links take you to the Web site of a "National Board of Education" (NBE) (www. nationalboardedu.com), which claims to be "recognized by the Education Ministry of the Republic of Liberia" and offers not only accreditation of education and training providers, but also services for individuals, including "degree evaluation," "degree authentication," "degree notarization," and "verification," all at a price.

In fact, NBE is associated with the infamous St. Regis University and other diploma mills run by individuals behind the St. Regis University operation, and has been declared fraudulent by the Embassy of Liberia in a statement posted on its Web site (www.embassyofliberia.org/news/item_a.html). A "who is" search discussed later shows that the NBE's domain name (www. nationalboardedu.com) is registered in Dominica, not Liberia. Further, on the bottom of each page on the NBE Web site, you will observe seals of the United Nations and The Great Seal of the United States next to the wording "United Nations Association of the United States of America and the Business Council for the United Nations." What does this kind of verbiage have to do with an education board that is supposed to be recognized in Liberia? Sounds too good to be true, doesn't it?

THE APOSTILLE

In the past year we have seen an increased effort by degree mills to portray their services (and issued documents) as legitimate, by recommending their customers the Apostille service. With the Apostille service, the documents (transcript, degree, etc.) are authenticated for use in another country through a notarization process. For details on the Apostille process, see LesLee Stedman's article, *Legalization: The Apostille* in the Summer 2001 (Vol. 77,

No. 1) issue of *College and University*, available online to AACRAO members at www.aacrao.org/publications/candu/index.cfm.

The Apostille process starts with having the foundation documents "notarized" by a local notary in the conventional manner, then at the county court level, state level, and finally by the United States Secretary of State. At each level, another sheet with ribbon and seal is added to the underlying documents. The fee for this process varies by state, from less than $1 to about $35.

This service is offered by St. Regis University for a fee of $1,800, whereas NBE only charges $1,200. Degree mills encourage the Apostille for persons using their transcripts and degrees abroad. As law enforcement has seen in the past (especially when Dr. Henry Kissinger was Secretary of State), persons

Figure 1. Various Diploma Mill School Listings

receiving these documents are blinded by the seals, ribbons, and signatures, and spend little time examining the underlying documents. Again, it's all camouflage.

Also, we have seen the increased use of foreign credential evaluation or validation services that are now used to further buttress degree mill documents as "equivalent to regionally-accredited u.s. or Canadian degrees." AACRAO International Education Services staff members have spotted questionable evaluation service Web sites that have "cloned" the Web pages of a long-standing and well-known evaluation service, have fabricated a quote by a leader in the field of foreign credential evaluation, and have even pirated the wording and format used by a highly-respected evaluation service to pass off as their own original product. Regrettably, we have also seen more than one such entity highlight its affiliation with AACRAO. Claiming "affiliation" with, "recognition" by, or membership in such organizations as AACRAO, NAFSA: Association of International Educators, EAIE (European Association for International Education), and other well-known, reputable, and authentic professional associations, is another attempt to give the impression of legitimacy.

How Do You Detect Fraudulent Transcripts?

Some institutions do not assign their more experienced personnel the task of handling transcripts and verifications. Like a teller in a bank, this is your first line of defense—this is where alertness, training, and experience come together. Catching the attempt to defraud your institution at this early stage can save you time, litigation, and embarrassment later.

Like an experienced bank teller who can detect counterfeit currency even when blindfolded, your frontline staff should have the skills and experience to be able to detect a fraudulent transcript, or at least become suspicious, just by the look and feel of the document. Here are questions to help you develop that sense that "something just isn't right."

◆ What is your first impression? What do your instincts tell you? Sometimes, you "just know" it's wrong.

◆ Are the fonts, horizontal, and vertical alignments correct? What does it look like?

◆ What is the quality of the paper?

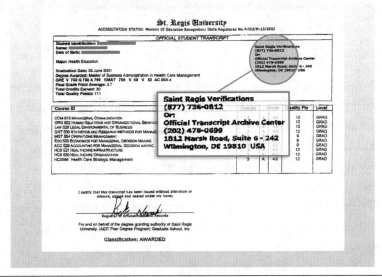

Figure 2A. Detecting Fraudulent Transcripts—Location of school and sender of documents differ in unusual ways (in this example, transcript for a "Liberian" school sent from an address in the U.S.)

Figure 2B. Detecting Fraudulent Transcripts—Return address of institution and postmark inconsistent in an unusual way

◆ Does the envelope bear the correct printed name and correct address of the issuing institution? Is the return address preprinted, is the address typed, or was a rubber stamp used?

◆ Was a postage stamp used on the envelope, or a postage meter machine with the name of the issuing institution?

◆ Does the document contain a current date, or is it "stale dated?" If "stale," where has it been?

◆ Is the registrar's signature and embossed university seal correct for this institution? If correct, are they crisp, clear, and legible?

◆ Was the document mailed directly from the registrar's office at the issuing institution, or is it from a third party? How was the envelope sealed?

◆ Is the overall appearance of this document similar to others you have previously seen from this same institution? Or does it appear to be remarkably similar to a transcript from a different university?

◆ Does this institution really exist? Is this school listed in your AACRAO Member Guide? Is it a regionally-accredited institution in the United States? What if it's a foreign school? Do you know how to confirm whether it is legitimate?

◆ Do the dates of birth, attendance, graduation, etc. match up? Do the courses correspond to the degree? Do the grades look right or was the student just "too good?"

(See Figures 2A and 2B on the previous page.)

What are Look-alikes and Sound-alikes?

A "look-alike" or "sound-alike" is any college or university (and accompanying Web site), which has been expressly established in a name similar to another institution in order to deceive potential students. You and your institution must be constantly vigilant for the fraudster who establishes a Web site with the name of your university or one that sounds very close to it.

For example, an individual set up his own Western Washington State University Web site (www.wwsu.edu [now defunct]), at which he welcomed students, claiming it was "the leader in distance learning education." Costs for degrees, with transcripts, were listed as $3,500 for a bachelor's degree, $4,500 for a master's degree, and $5,000 for a Ph.D. Naturally, as designed, some individuals confused this Web site with the real university Web site for Western Washington State University in Bellingham, Washington (www.wwu.edu). When confronted by personnel of the legitimate Western Washington State University, the only thing the fraudster did was change the name of his entity to Western Washington International University. He kept the same Web address, and continued his business.

"Who Is" the Owner of That Web Site?

An Internet "who is" search of an IP (Internet protocol) of a Web site URL can be a helpful tool to determine or identify the owner of a Web site or the party responsible for content or technical support on a Web site. For example, a

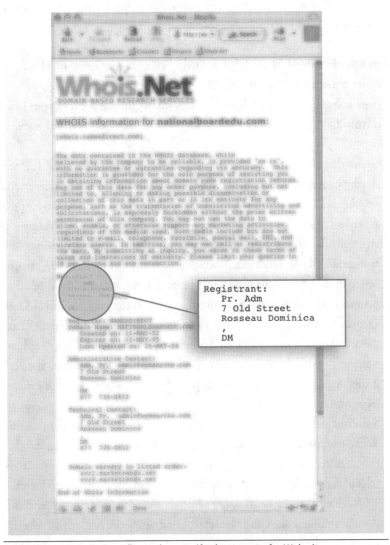

Figure 3. Example "Who-is" search to verify the owner of a Web site

"who is" search using the Web site www.whois.net shows that the domain of the National Board of Education (NBE), www.nationalboardedu.com, which claims to be "recognized by the Education Ministry of the Republic of Liberia," is registered at 7 Old Street, Rosseau, Dominica, not in Liberia (see Figure 3 on the previous page). This should send up a red flag about the identity of this organization. You might want to do an Internet search for your school's name to see if you find any "look-alikes" or "sound-alikes," and if you do, do a "who is" search for the registrant of the domain name. It is a first step in protecting your institution's name and reputation.

How Do I Prevent Transcript Fraud? What is My Role in This?

I believe these two questions should be addressed together.

You have a duty to yourself and to your institution to prevent your institution from being victimized. Again, *be proactive*! *Your institution's name is at risk.*

◆ Insist that your institution, (if they have not previously done so), trademark your school seal, logo, name, etc. Thus when anyone sells counterfeit degrees or transcripts in the name of your institution, it is an automatic violation of the Trademark Statute (18 U.S.C. 2320). When used properly, this statute can have a chilling effect on counterfeiters, as evidenced by the action of University of Notre Dame officials (via the U.S. Attorney's office and the FBI), resulting in the prosecution of an individual doing business as USSI/BACD (Unlimited Success Strategies, Inc./Buy A College Degree), Sunrise, Florida. He was prosecuted in United States District Court, Southern District of Florida, for violation of the Trademark Statute relative to his manufacture and sale of degrees and transcripts under the name of Notre Dame. (He also offered hundreds of other colleges and universities.)

◆ Your institution has clout with both state and federal prosecutors—use it. Write them a letter, file a complaint, and let your voice be heard.

◆ Be alert for persons selling not only degrees and transcripts in your school's name, but also offering rubber stamps, seals, security paper, and other means of authenticating your school's documents. When any of these fraudulent activities are detected, identify the persons offering these items for sale, and then do something about it.

WHAT DO I DO? HOW DO I DO IT?

◆ **Do your research.** Find out what's for sale. In an effort to "build your case," do your research on what the fraudster is actually offering. You should consider buying at least one of each of the items being offered for sale under your institution's name. In this manner, you will be able to recognize the source of some of the fraudulent items that are presented to your institution for verification. Also, be sure to save all envelopes in which these items were delivered to you, as all these items will be later used as evidence, in either threatened litigation, litigation, or by law enforcement in criminal prosecution.

◆ **Now, take action against the fraudster.** Do this on behalf of your institution, or on behalf of all schools facing a similar situation. Your action can be as simple as your attorney sending the fraudster a "cease and desist" letter, with copies directed to your state's attorney general, the FBI, U.S. Postal Inspector, etc. Your letter can be similar to the "Gotcha Letter" shown in Figure 4. The fraudster will get the message. If for some reason this has no effect on him/her, consider litigation.

◆ **Demand action from law enforcement.** Once you and your institution have done your parts, it is up to you to demand that local/state/federal law enforcement do theirs. Demand that they do something. Keep up the pressure by frequently calling the assigned investigator or the prosecutor. Let them know of your institution's continued interest and that your institution is paying attention. Demand results. If you are successful in getting a case prosecuted, make time in your schedule to attend each court hearing. Each jurisdiction has its own rules regarding "victim witness." Normally, the District Attorney's office will complete a form that will be given to the judge hearing the case. Thus, the judge knows that your institution is represented in court and is watching for results. At the time of sentencing, most jurisdictions will offer the victim witness a chance to address the court if there is anything he or she desires to say prior to sentencing. This will be your chance to advise the court if this person has been cooperative or not, has identified his supplier of the counterfeit documents, and of the harm done to your institution. *This is your chance to stand up and be heard.*

How Do You Handle Fraudulent Documents?

◆ Handle/touch the documents as little as possible. Place each original document in a plastic sleeve in order to protect latent fingerprints, original ink signatures/rubber stamps, and printing/typewriting.

◆ Once the original is in plastic, make a working copy to use in lieu of the original.

◆ Retain the original envelope in which you received the fraudulent document. Treat in the same manner as above. This is your only evidence as to how you received the document, and the use of the United States Mail (a violation of the Mail Fraud Statute [18 U.S.C. 1341]).

◆ Date and initial the reverse side of all documents/envelopes.

◆ If faxed documents are involved, save the original fax. The fax header line identifies the sender's fax machine, and thus is the evidence needed to show if the fax traveled in interstate commerce (Fraud By Wire Statute [18 U.S.C. 1343]).

◆ Retain all fraudulent documents in a secure location for later "chain of custody" by law enforcement. (They will inquire as to where the document has been, and who has had possession since it was received.)

Dear [fraud suspect]:

The purpose of this letter is to inform you of the [telephone call or letter] which we received from [current/prospective employer or education institution] in their effort to verify your education credentials. We were advised you had indicated you were a graduate of [school name] and you may have submitted documents to support your graduation from [school name].

Since we are unable to locate any record of your graduation from our institution, we have so advised those persons attempting to verify your purported education credentials.

We hereby request you cease and desist your assertion that you are a graduate of this institution and request you destroy any and all documents which you may have created or purchased indicating your graduation from our institution.

As you appear to be using fraudulent credentials—which may be in violation of various local, state, and federal statutes—we have referred this matter to our university attorney. Additionally, a copy of this letter has been furnished to the FBI and U.S. Postal Inspector for any action they deem appropriate.

Figure 4. Sample "Gotcha Letter" Language

Deterrents to Transcript Fraud:
Devalue the Product and Eliminate the Source

I believe the same approach to degree fraud should be taken with transcript fraud—*devalue the product and eliminate the source*. By doing this, the laws of supply and demand will take effect.

◆ **Embarrass and prosecute those using fictitious transcripts.** Should law enforcement execute a search warrant on your false credential case, ensure they understand your desire to obtain a listing of any and all persons who purchase degrees and transcripts in the name of your institution. In all my cases as an FBI agent, as each case was adjudicated in Untied States District Court, the Assistant United States Attorney placed into the court record a computerized listing of all persons purchasing such degrees and transcripts, along with their addresses, type of degree/transcript purchased, date on document, etc., thus making it a "public record."

This public document was then immediately available both to any interested college or university, and to the press. To make it more enticing, these listings were alphabetical, by state of residence, and by degree type. Thus, it was easy to identify persons purchasing a degree in a specific area, such as Education, Law Enforcement, or Medicine. This document was a big hit with the press. Several stories appeared in *The Chronicle of Higher Education*, and other publications, in which they listed the identities of these graduates. Publicity and the resulting humiliation for the purchasers serve as a strong public deterrent, and devalue the product.

> In an effort to educate its members, AACRAO has encouraged presentations at state, regional, and national meetings on both degree mills and transcript fraud. Further, AACRAO regularly sponsors workshops and presentations on degree mill/transcript fraud and publishes resources on best practices in the security and review of academic records, including the book *Misrepresentation in the Marketplace and Beyond: Ethics under Siege*, ed. Peggy Askins, 1996. See the AACRAO Web site at www.aacrao.org for more information on publications and professional development opportunities.

◆ **At the same time, stop the transcript mill when it first opens.** Do not let it establish a presence in the marketplace. If it sells degrees and transcripts of your college or university (or templates containing your blank degrees and transcripts), then consult your university counsel and the Attorney

General's office for prosecution, or as an alternative, for a cease and desist order. *Stop them immediately.*

With diligence on the part of higher education professionals, the business and employment community, government service agencies, and law enforcement officials, the problem of fraudulent transcripts, and credential fraud overall, can be addressed, and hopefully eradicated in the near future. For this to happen, we each must get involved and do our part. *Be a part of the solution, not the problem!*

✗✗✗✗✗✗✗✗✗✗✗✗✗✗✗✗

CHAPTER FIVE

Bogus High Schools in the United States

by Jessica Montgomery

T he proliferation of fraudulent secondary institutions in the United States has arisen from a disturbing development in the intelligence and organization behind these operations. While not as rampant as postsecondary diploma mills, these "schools" are similarly established by profit-driven men and women, many with a criminal history. Fraudulent high schools both impede unknowing students who, without an authentic high school education, find themselves at a significant disadvantage in the work force and in pursuing further education; and they detract from the employment opportunities available to individuals with a legitimate high school diploma.

This epidemic falls into two categories: fraudulent schools that operate without the students' or parents' knowledge and diploma mills patronized by dishonest consumers. As demonstrated by recent cases in New York, Florida and California, those most affected by high school fraud are low-income and immigrant families.

A case in Florida drew attention to the problem of high school diploma mills through its disclosure of certain issues surrounding academic eligibility for athletes. University High School in Miami was investigated and exposed for providing fraudulent education and subsequently shut down. Initial attention was brought to the school's practices by an article in the *New York Times* reporting that the school, officially a correspondence school, had no teachers and administered open-book tests. University High School conferred degrees for approximately $300 to $400 each to high school athletes with grade problems, as well as to its main clientele of dropouts and immigrants. Florida state law prohibits the regulation of private schools, possibly concealing more similar cases.

The investigation into University High School found that the students who obtained their diplomas through University High and subsequently attended college—many of them to play sports—were not prepared for the level of work and either dropped out or were banned from playing sports. More than a dozen athletes gained eligibility from the National Collegiate Athletic Association (NCAA) through their degrees from University High School prompting the NCAA to name a panel to investigate the various nontraditional avenues used by students to secure college scholarships and academic eligibility in athletics.

The founder of University High School, Stanley J. Simmons, spent ten months in prison in the 1980s after being associated with a diploma mill. Simmons' exploits were initially uncovered by Allan Ezell, then in charge of the FBI's Operation Dipscam and presently head of corporate security for Wachovia Corporation. Mr. Simmons sold the school to its manager Michael R. Kinney approximately two years ago.

In recent years the state of New York has cracked down on many cases of fraudulent schools claiming to be accredited or to offer some legitimate educational product. The GE Career Center, Inc. (GECC) operating out of Queens used false and misleading advertisements and telephone solicitations to induce consumers into paying $100–$150 for the General Educational Development Diploma (GED). From 1999 to 2002, GECC offered a correspondence course, targeting high school dropouts with the opportunity to receive study materials and take the GED test at home. In a lawsuit brought by New York Attorney General Eliot Spitzer in October 2002, the judge ruled that the Center refund thousands of dollars to customers. Referring to the high school equivalency correspondence course as "a deliberate, well-organized and planned attempt to mislead the public," Justice Leland DeGrasse barred GECC from offering or selling their GED preparation course.

Spitzer's office began its investigation when nearly sixty individuals contacted the attorney general's office to complain that GECC staff misled them into believing that the test being offered was official or that they paid for services but received nothing in return. In addition, consumers who received materials and took the test soon discovered that the "diploma" issued by GECC was worthless when they applied to a college or for a job.

Similarly, in March 2001, Attorney General Eliot Spitzer sued Harlem International Community School (HICS) for falsely representing to parents that it was authorized to issue high school diplomas and administer Board of Regents exams. New York state law does allow high schools to operate without a charter, but they cannot issue diplomas without being registered with the Board of Regents. The school was originally chartered in 1977 as a grade school, under the name of Lower East Side International Community School. In its representation as a high school, it required parents to pay extravagant fees, including a nonrefundable application fee of $750, $3,000 per year for tuition and $500 for building maintenance. Says Senator David Patterson, who notified Spitzer of the consumer complaints: "It is inconceivable that HICS officials would prey on the hard-working parents of this community who, like all of us, only want the best for our children."

Another case in Harlem opened in March 2005, when Spitzer again announced a lawsuit confronting a fraudulent school, the Harlem Youth Enrichment Christian Academy. Its founder, Andre C. McNair, opened the center in September, 2001, advertising to the Harlem community that the school was accredited by the New York State Board of Regents and that it offered various academic and extracurricular activities. After an investigation by the Office of the Attorney General, it was found that McNair falsely claimed to be a physician and graduate of Fordham University and the University of Medicine and Dentistry in New Jersey and that he did postgraduate work at other accredited institutions. In reality, he spent only a few semesters at Fordham without graduating and the other institutions have no record of his attendance.

In 2002–2003, the school charged parents—many of them of modest means—$3,250 annually and $350 per month. The Academy closed abruptly on February 14, 2003 after failing to provide the academic and extracurricular activities advertised. Parents never received tuition refunds. Assemblyman

Keith Wright (D-Harlem) commented: "What is most disturbing is the way these individuals operating the academy manipulated a trusting Harlem community and parents who understand the value and absolute necessity of a quality education in uplifting a young man or woman's life."

One recently resolved case concerns the Academy at Ivy Ridge in Ogdensburg, New York, a school targeting troubled youth. The school was required to pay a fine of $250,000 and to provide 15 percent tuition refunds to the families of the 113 graduates of the academy who had paid on average $50,000 in tuition. It also agreed to stop issuing and advertising its false high school diplomas. The school claimed to be accredited by the Northwest Association of Accredited Schools, but was actually only being considered for accreditation. The investigation was prompted by complaints from parents beginning in 2004. The school's Web site, academyivyridge.com, now states that they are not accredited and not authorized by the New York State Department of Education to confer diplomas or administer Board of Regents exams.

The California Alternative High School (CAHS) conducted classes in approximately thirty locations in California, as well as at least twelve other states. The school targeted a mainly Hispanic population, persuading them that a CAHS diploma would help them gain admission to college and obtain financial aid. CAHS also marketed itself as fulfilling the American Dream of escaping poverty, while charging up to $1450 for a ten-week, thirty-hour course. The students were also given workbooks, containing numerous factual errors, including a statement that the United States consists of fifty-three states and that the United States government has four branches and two houses—one for Democrats and one for Republicans. California Attorney General Bill Lockyer sued the school in 2004 and reached a settlement of $500,000.

The many recent cases of fraudulent secondary education raise crucial questions. How easily should private institutions be authorized to advertise as a secondary school without an investigation into the authenticity of the education offered? How involved should state or federal governments be in the assessment of secondary education? What legal steps should be taken to prosecute and punish those responsible for operating these bogus institutions? It is also difficult in some cases to prove that the individual obtaining false credentials was aware of the institution's criminality. This raises another question about the nature of prosecution—what level of responsibility should the consumer assume?

Certainly students' families should be educated about the possibility of fraudulent education and given the tools to recognize suspicious institutions. They should look for state or organizational accreditation and verify that accreditation with the corresponding agency, as well as confirm the validity of the accrediting body. Many diploma mills will list bogus accreditations and some even establish their own illegitimate accrediting agencies. Although many of these "schools" use the Internet to market their fraudulent product, the Internet's vast resources can also aid aware consumers in investigating dubious claims.

The Web site of the Federal Trade Commission provides guidance for identifying fraudulent credentials. Some of the warning signs include degrees earned out of sequence, degrees obtained in an unusually short time, degrees earned from institutions located away from an individual's job or home and credentials received from institutions with names similar to those of well-known institutions.

The existence of diploma mills on both the secondary and postsecondary level has far reaching consequences. As revealed in an article by Clay Risen in *The New Republic*, diploma mills not only hurt vulnerable families, but they can be a national security risk when false records are used to obtain government jobs. In addition, individuals with bogus qualifications can take jobs away from those with legitimately earned degrees and, as a result, reduce the value of education in general. When individuals with inadequate backgrounds enter the workforce, tragedy can result. In 2002, a North Carolina doctor with a degree from a diploma mill was implicated in the death of an eight-year-old patient. Unfortunately, the problem of diploma mills is not addressed with a view to these greater effects—as Alan Ezell noted in *The Miami Herald*: "It's seen as a white-collar, victimless crime. They think there's no victim. No blood."

Bibliography

Consumeraffairs.com. 2005. Bogus california high schools to pay $500,000. 18 March. Available at: <www.consumeraffairs.com/news04/2005/cahs_settlement.html>.
Federal Trade Commission. 2005 (January). *Avoid Fake-degree Burns by Researching Academic Credentials*. Available at: <www.ftc.gov/bcp/conline/pubs/buspubs/diplomamills.htm>.

Grimm, Fred. 2005a. Diploma mill for dumb jocks: wink-wink. *Miami Herald.* 1 December. Available at: <www.miami.com/mld/miamiherald/news/columnists/fred_grimm/13296828 .htm>.

———. 2005b. Diploma scams victim-free until someone is hurt. *Miami Herald.* 4 December. Available at: <www.miami.com/mld/miamiherald/13315489.htm>.

Lederman, Doug. 2005. NCAA to study high school policies. *Inside Higher Ed.* 28 December. Available at: <http://insidehighered.com/news/2005/12/28/ncaa>.

Office of New York State Attorney General Eliot Spitzer. 2001. Spitzer Sues Harlem High School for Fraud (press release). 29 March. Available at: <www.oag.state.ny.us/press/2001/ mar/mar29b_01.html>.

———. 2002. Judge Slams Queens-Based High School Equivalency Exam (press release). October 25, 2002. Available at: <www.oag.state.ny.us/press/2002/oct/oct25a_02.html>.

Risen, Clay. 2006. The Scourge of Fake Diplomas. Degree Burns. *The New Republic Online.* 17 January. Available at: <www.tnr.com/doc.mhtml?i=20060123&s=risen012306>.

Thamel, Pete and D. Wilson. 2005. Poor grades aside, athletes get into college on a $399 diploma. *New York Times.* 27 November. Available at: <www.doubleazone.com/ November%2027.htm>.

Wilson, Duff. 2005. Florida School in sports case will shut down under pressure. *New York Times.* 24 December. Available at: <www.doubleazone.com/uhigh.htm>.

◇◇◇◇◇◇◇◇◇◇◇◇◇◇◇◇◇◇◇◇

CHAPTER SIX

Diploma Mills:
The $200-Million-a-Year
Competitor You Didn't
Know You Had

by John Bear

For the sake of argument, let's say you run the company that makes Rolex watches. For many years, your company has carefully cultivated and protected its reputation for quality. One day you pick up a major business magazine and see the following advertisement: "Genuine Rolex Watches by Mail, $50." You quickly learn that they are being made in a huge factory in another country. You are confident that your sales will be dramatically affected, and as these fakes fail to work well, your reputation will be damaged. But despite your increasingly frantic attempts, you are unable to interest law enforcement agencies in taking any action, and you can't persuade the media to stop running those ads.

It sounds like a nightmare.

It is a nightmare, and it's happening today—not in the world of wristwatches, but in the world of higher education. Consider the following:

◆ There are more than 300 unaccredited universities now operating. While a few are genuine start-ups or online ventures, the great majority range from merely dreadful to out-and-out diploma mills—fake schools that will sell people any degree they want at prices from $3,000 to $5,000.

◆ It is not uncommon for a large fake school to "award" as many as 500 Ph.D.s every month.

- The aggregate income of the bad guys is easily in excess of $200 million a year. Data show that a single phony school can earn between $10 million and $20 million annually.
- With the closure of the FBI's diploma mill task force, the indifference of most state law enforcement agencies, the minimal interest of the news media, and the growing ease of using the Internet to start and run a fake university, things are rapidly growing worse.

The prognosis is bleak. This is not some jerk with a laser printer on his kitchen table cranking out a few phony diplomas, often to the mild amusement of the media (as when Florida congressman Claude Pepper bought a fake doctorate to show how easy it was and proclaimed himself Dr. Pepper). Fake schools are a serious economic force in America, hitting legitimate schools in their pocketbooks in two important ways:

- A fair chunk of that $200 million is being spent by people who really want and need a legitimate degree but don't know enough to tell the difference. It's tuition that should be going to the legitimate schools.
- Every time a phony school is exposed by the media, the whole public perception of distance learning suffers. So when the public sees your ad or press release, they are more likely to say, sneeringly, "Oh, I've heard about those kinds of programs," and you'll never hear from them.

A huge crime wave is under way, and almost no one has noticed. You can't have a crime wave without two basic ingredients: villains and victims. In this particular crime wave, there are four kinds of villains and four kinds of victims. In the course of looking at each of them, much can be learned about what is going on, and why.

The Four Villains

Who are the villains in this sad drama? There is an obvious one (the perpetrators), a less obvious one (the customers), and two very important ones: the media and law enforcement.

Of course there would be no such institutions without these people, and we cannot excuse their behavior. They were not sold into the diploma trade. No, they all know precisely what they are doing, and they are doing it for money and, perhaps, the prestige that comes with a business card reading "University President."

These folks typically fall into three categories: Lifelong scam artists, who might have progressed from three-card monte on the street corner to running a university; quirky academics who have decided to cross to the dark side; and businesspeople who simply find another kind of business—that of selling degrees.

An example of one such businessman is James Kirk. In addition to dabbling in film production, 3-D film distribution, and a video dating service, in the late 70s he got involved with a correspondence law school called the University of San Gabriel Valley (it no longer exists; the California Supreme Court suspended one of Kirk's lawyer-partners for three years and placed the other on probation for a year). But Kirk saw the cash potential and opened his own Southland University down the street. When Southland could no longer meet California's minimal operating requirements, he moved it. It ended up in Missouri, where he changed its name to LaSalle University and his own to Thomas McPherson. Leaving Missouri a few steps ahead of the sheriff, he found a haven in Louisiana's unregulated world of higher education. He ran ads in dozens of airline and business magazines. He took a vow of poverty, so his World Christian Church owned the university, his Porsche, and his million-dollar home. And when the federal authorities finally came for him, they discovered bank deposits in excess of $35 million, current cash deposits of $10 million, and numerous other assets. Kirk/McPherson was indicted on 18 counts of mail fraud, wire (telephone) fraud, and tax fraud, among others. Following a plea bargain, he was sentenced to five years in federal prison.

What is he up to now? Well shortly after he arrived at the federal pen in Beaumont, Texas, a new university started advertising nationally. The Edison University campus in Honolulu turned out to be a Mail Boxes Etc. box rental store. The literature was almost identical to that of LaSalle. The registrar was one Natalie Handy, James Kirk's wife. And the mail was postmarked

Beaumont, Texas. Instead of "University Without Walls," we may well have a case here of "University Behind Bars."

One of the academics who has gone down this path is Dr. Mary Rodgers, founder and president of the Open University of America. She has an earned doctorate from Ohio State and had a decent career in higher education. When I visited the, um, campus, I found it to be a pleasant suburban home in Maryland. When a young girl answered the door, I said I was looking for Open University. "She's upstairs," was the reply. When I asked Dr. Rodgers about the legitimacy of the university, she showed me photos of their graduation ceremony at the National Shrine of the Immaculate Conception in Washington D.C., featuring mostly, it seemed, foreign military officers receiving their degrees. "What more could you ask for?" she inquired. Oh, perhaps something more than grandma in the basement (I had been given a tour) filling orders.

Then there's lifelong con-man Ronald Pellar (aka Ronald Dante), undisputed king of the fraudulent school world, who probably has tens of millions of dollars in offshore bank accounts to prove it. Following an early career as a Las Vegas lounge hypnotist, a brief stint as Lana Turner's seventh and last husband (she threw him out and accused him of robbery), and a two-year prison stretch for hiring a hit man to kill someone, Pellar discovered the world of education and training. He also hit upon the easiest method yet of becoming a "Doctor." He called himself Doctor Dante. After making a bundle with his fake travel-agent training school and his dangerous cosmetology school (he was convicted under federal fair trade laws in California for running the fake cosmetology school), he hit the big time with his Columbia State University. Starting in the late 1980s from a Mail Boxes Etc. store in New Orleans and featuring a Ph.D. in 27 days—no questions asked—Columbia State University grew and grew. By 1997 Pellar had several employees filling orders in an unmarked warehouse in San Clemente, California, not far from the Nixon museum. Between January 1997 and March 1998, according to the New Orleans Times-Picayune, the school deposited approximately $16 million in its bank account. By this time, Pellar was living on his million-dollar yacht in Ensenada, Mexico, defying warrants for his arrest. In 2000, Pellar gave a rather smug interview from the deck of his yacht to ABC's 20/20, making fun of the stupidity of his "clients." Shortly afterward, he was arrested on re-entering the United States, and imprisoned for his *previous* fraud, the Permaderm Institute, which purported to teach people how to apply permanent make-up using tattoos. (They practiced using ball point pens on cantaloupes!) In 2003, he was indicted on eight counts of fraud for his Columbia State activities, and in April 2004 he was sentenced to seven years in prison (but the judge inexplicably deducted 6 years and 4 months from the sentence for time previously served on the unrelated offenses, which included the fake school, witness intimidation, jury tampering, and escape). So Pellar will be serving only eight months in prison for fleecing thousands of people out of millions of dollars. The FBI was not able to find any of his assets other than his $1.5 million yacht, and while the court ordered it confiscated, it is in international waters, and may not be easy to recover.

The obvious question at this point is: How could he make so much money, for so long, with such a blatantly phony (to you and me, at least) scheme? The answer can be found by looking at the other three categories of villains.

VILLAIN #2: THE MEDIA

No fraudulent scheme can succeed if people don't know about it. And the traditional way to make yourself known, whether you are selling Coca-Cola or doctorates, is to advertise.

Pellar's basic advertisement for Columbia State University read like this:

University Degree in 27 Days!
Bachelor's, Master's, Doctorate
Legal, legitimate, and fully accredited.
School rings available.

What publication on Earth, with the possible exception of the supermarket tabloids, would run such an ad? Well, how about the *Economist, Time, Newsweek, Forbes, Money, Business Week, Investors Business Daily*, and *USA Today*?

Surely, the rational mind asks, no responsible publication would continue to run such ads, once they learned the nature of the advertiser. But the media I contacted reacted in one of three ways when they learned they'd been running advertisements for fraudulent schools.

◆ **We run them. Period.** The *Economist* is one of the worst offenders: Every weekly issue for at least the last five years has had five to 20 ads for "schools" that range from to tally phony to merely unaccredited and bad. Because of the magazine's excellent reputation, many readers assume if a school advertises in the Economist, it must be OK. When I first tugged at the magazine's sleeve, sending them clear evidence of their bogus advertisers, the response from Suzanne Hopkins in their classified ad department was loud and clear: "Although I understand your urgency of making people aware of the dealings of Columbia State University, we are of the belief that our readers are educated enough to make there [sic] own decisions." (As a conservative guess, readers lost over a million dollars to this one phony alone, before the FBI finally closed it down.)

We run them. Wait, no we won't. Many years ago, the Wall Street Journal was running some ads for reprehensible schools. My attempts at getting their attention either went unanswered or elicited replies like that from Hopkins. Then one day, when an especially dreadful ad appeared, I went into my "terrier" mode (relentless, get teeth in and don't let go). I finally got through to the key decision maker in New York. Robert Higgins, of their advertising standards committee said, in effect, "Of course we shouldn't be doing this," and they simply stopped. It was simple because they said what any medium could say: "If a school doesn't have recognized accreditation, we don't run their ads. Period."

We won't run them. Wait; yes we will. For sheer numbers, *USA Today* is the champ. Every morning, the flagship of the Gannett fleet runs from five to 15 ads from questionable schools in the Education section of their classified page, although sometimes the ads migrate into the rest of the paper, notably, one full-page ad (at an estimated $70,000) for a phony university. When I did my sleeve-tugging act at *USA Today*, the response was immediate and gratifying. Cynthia Ross, in the advertising office, seemed genuinely alarmed and promptly drew up a set of standards and guidelines for accepting school ads, which were as reasonable and rigorous as anything I would have done. She thanked me profusely and assured me that changes would be implemented as soon as questionnaires were sent to advertisers. The only problem is that this happened three years ago, no changes were made, and Ross no longer returns my calls.

Another failing of the media is indifference. The two-headed snake at the 4-H show will probably get more coverage than the local high school principal discovered to have a fake degree. Or the campaign literature of former senator Joseph Biden reporting a degree he didn't have. Or the president of Croatia with a worthless California doctorate. Or Arizona's "teacher of the year" with a bogus master's. Is this business as usual? The press hardly noticed. When the FBI discovered that a few scientists at NASA had fake doctorates, the news was largely ignored by the press. When the Fowler family—some of the most flamboyant degree mill operators ever—were charged with stealing millions and put on trial in North Carolina, the courthouse was full of reporters, but only because Jim and Tammy Faye Bakker and Fawn Hall were on trial in the next room. Despite the best efforts of the FBI and yours truly, not an inch of copy ever appeared.

VILLAIN #3: THE WORLD OF LAW ENFORCEMENT

If I held up a 7-Eleven for 50 bucks, I'd probably be in prison before my Slurpee melted. But if I start a totally fraudulent university, selling degrees by return mail for $3,000 each, and I obscure my path just a little, changing the name from time to time and using various mail-forwarding services, the odds are that I will go unpunished forever. And if caught, I will get little more than a slap on the wrist.

Because of the multistate and international aspect of many fakes, it's often unclear who has jurisdiction. When, as in the case of one huge fraud, a man in California rents a one-room "campus" in Utah and mails his diplomas from Hawaii, who regulates him? In the Columbia State saga, for years the attorney general of Louisiana was saying, in effect, "He may use a mail drop here, but the entire operation is run from California. It's their problem." And the California attorney general was saying, "Hey, he uses a Louisiana address and telephone in all his ads and in his catalog. It's their problem."

In this great republic of ours, each state has its own school licensing laws, and they differ mightily and change regularly. During the 1990s more new universities opened in Hawaii than in the rest of the country combined: over 100 of them, and all but two or three located at mailbox service addresses. In the 1980s it was Louisiana, a state that did not license degree-granting institutions. Recently, the state of choice for this kind of thing has been South Dakota.

It wasn't always this way. In 1980 the FBI made diploma mills a priority and established the DipScam task force, based in Charlotte, North Carolina. With the states generally uninterested in acting, time after time the FBI did the research, secured a search warrant, marched in (often with postal inspectors and the IRS in tow), collected evidence, got indictments, and ended up closing down more than 50 major frauds, including two active fake medical schools.

But in the early 1990s FBI agent Allen Ezell, scourge of the degree mills, took early retirement, and the agency removed diploma mills from its priority list. The sad news is that more fakes and near-fakes have been launched in the last 10 years than in the previous 50. They are fueled by the ease of advertising and the even greater ease of setting up an impressive-looking Internet site—even one with the hallowed .edu suffix, which many people think signifies quality, but which has been doled out to many questionable schools.

There have been a few good guys in the last few years-but not many. One assistant attorney general in Illinois guards his state like a bulldog. When a fake Loyola State University opened not far from the real Loyola University in Chicago, Assistant Attorney General Hollister Bundy got an injunction and closed them down within a few days. But Attorney General Richard Ieyoub of Louisiana yawned and looked the other way for years, until a close election battle in 1998 spurred him to action, posing for photos while shutting down a few notorious mailboxes. And California's top lawman showed zero interest while some of the biggest frauds ever thumbed their noses in the direction of Sacramento.

Even when some action is taken, it may not be enough. Since 1998 the Federal Trade Commission has had the important power to regulate the use of the word "accredited," but to my knowledge, it has never filed a case, despite blatant misuse of that word. In 1997, the state of California ordered Columbia Pacific University to close but the "university" appealed and remained defiantly open for nearly four more years, continuing to advertise nationally. In

2001, as its appeals ran out, it moved to Missoula, Montana, changed its name to Commonwealth Pacific University, and remains in business.

VILLAIN #4: THE PEOPLE WHO BUY AND USE FAKE DEGREES

The question is always asked: Do the customers of these schools know what they're doing? Are they acquiring what they are well aware is a questionable degree for the purpose of fooling others? Or have they genuinely been fooled by the purveyor of the parchment?

The only certain answer is that there are some of each, but whether it is 50-50 or any other proportion is quite unknown and much discussed. Surely, you are thinking, anyone with an IQ higher than room temperature who acquires that "Ph.D. in 27 days" must know exactly what he or she is doing. And yet. And yet, the literature and the sales pitch of the phony Columbia State is really slick. The catalog is more attractive than some real schools, replete with photos of campus scenes, happy alumni (all from stock photo companies) and two Nobel laureates listed with honorary doctorates.

Their argument is that many universities today are giving credit for experiential learning. If you've run a business for 10 years, they suggest, you know more than most M.B.A.s (heads nod), and so we'll give you that M.B.A. If you've taught Sunday School at church, you know as much as one of those Ivy League doctors of divinity, and we'll award you the degree you've already earned through experience.

When I put a detailed exposé of Columbia State up on my Web site, I received more than 500 replies from alumni. While most were of the boy-was-I-stupid sort, a significant subset were like the woman who wrote, "I can't believe I did this. I have a master's degree from Goddard [College in Vermont]. I really understand this 'life experience' thing. Those people were sooo convincing."

And, depressingly, there was another notable subset of people who said, "Well if they're as bad as you say, how come my employer (they name a Fortune 500 company) is paying for three of us to do that degree?"

My hunch is that at least half the "victims" are truly co-conspirators. They know they live in a world where employers pay higher salary for the same job if the person has a higher degree; where therapists with a Ph.D. after their name are said to get three times as many Yellow Pages responses as those with an M.A.; and where a large Ohio city told the man who had been cutting down dead trees for them for 20 years that, due to a new policy, unless he earned a degree within two years, he would be let go. So they're willing to take the risk.

Surely it would be nice to see some meaningful research about these matters. I believe that I am right when I tell people, as I have for years, that using such a degree is like putting a time bomb in their resumè. One never knows when it might go off with dire effects. In my expert-witness work, I see this all the time. A few years ago, for instance, I testified against a prison psychologist for the state of Florida who had gotten away with his fake Ph.D. for eight years. He insisted that he believed the University of England was real, in spite of their P.O. box address, the absence of a telephone, and their offer to backdate his diploma to the year of his choice. As the prosecutor said in summation, "Here is a man who probably spent more time deciding which candy to buy from the vending machine than he did in choosing his doctoral school."

The Four Victims

VICTIM #1: THOSE BUYERS WHO AREN'T VILLAINS

And many of them aren't. Some stories introduced at diploma mill trials are heartbreaking: old people mortgaging their homes to provide their children's tuition; people selling their cars to pay their fees; and untold numbers of people losing their jobs, even being fined, jailed, or, if holding a green card, deported, for unwitting use of fake degrees.

VICTIM #2: THE EMPLOYERS

Employers are victimized in two ways: The obvious one is ending up with untrained employees, and the more subtle but potentially devastating one is financial liability when people with fake credentials make mistakes that damage people or property. Consider the urgent meetings that must have taken place when a prominent staff pediatrician at the University of California–Berkeley student health center was discovered to have forged his medical degree. A matter that sometimes keeps me up at night is two sleazy (but excessively litigious) universities that specialize in quick and easy home-study doctorates in nuclear engineering safety.

How can such things happen? Many employers either don't check or don't care. LaSalle University in Louisiana, shortly before their founder went to prison for mail fraud, listed hundreds of companies that they said had accepted and paid for their degrees. Skeptically, I started calling these companies, fully expecting to find the "university" had lied. But they hadn't. About half the companies had confused them with the real LaSalle University in Philadelphia. And the rest believed their accreditation claim, because they didn't realize there was such a thing as fake accreditation.

VICTIM #3: THE PUBLIC

Many well-meaning people suffer because the person they think is a trained teacher, business consultant, or engineer may not have the degree or even the knowledge. Consider the damage potential of the sex therapist in Syracuse with his fake Ph.D., for which he paid $100. The import-export lawyer in San Francisco who turned out to have bought his University of Michigan law degree from one of the insidious, no-questions-asked, "lost" diploma replacement services that advertise nationally. This spring, I'm scheduled to testify in California Superior Court, to help expose the phony doctorate claimed by the expert witness for the plaintiff. This man's Ph.D., his only degree, is from a well-known European "university." But for more than 20 years, this worthless credential has buttressed his scientific testimony in more than 300 court cases. If we are successful, it could lead to reopening all those other cases. And that's just one person from one "school." We are truly talking about the tiniest tip of a very large iceberg.

VICTIM #4: THE LEGITIMATE SCHOOLS

Just as the fake Rolex seller harms legitimate watch companies by taking money that should be theirs and by tarnishing their reputations, the fake schools take millions from the good schools' pockets, and, at least as significantly, foul the waters of nontraditional higher education.

Despite the huge surge of interest and investment in online and distance learning, everything is not rosy in the groves of virtual academe. Extremely well funded efforts such as California Virtual University just couldn't attract enough students and faded away. How many potential students were on the verge of sending for a catalog or writing a check to a good school when they saw one of the fake school exposés on 20/20, 60 Minutes, or Inside Edition, and decided not to take the risk of dealing with "one of those" schools.

What can legitimate schools do?

If there were an Olympic gold medal for hand-wringing, the foes of diploma mills would have won one years ago. But, with the lone exception of the FBI's decade-long effort, results have been sporadic, generally ineffective, and woefully short-lived. In 1982 the American Council on Education announced an impending, hard-hitting, and uncompromising book (I hoped) on fake schools. But by the time *Diploma Mills: Degrees of Fraud* finally emerged in 1988, the lawyers had marched in, and the book was, at best, soft-hitting and compromised. The authors apologized for lack of specificity (not a single currently operating fake was named) because of "the present litigious era."

Yes, schools do sue. When *Lingua Franca*, the sister publication of *University Business*, ran an article about Mellon University Press and Mellon University (which they judged to be a diploma mill), they were sued by the owner. They ultimately prevailed in court, but it was a long, expensive process. I've been sued eight times by schools, including once, for $500 million, by the University of North America. Only one ever got to court, and that was thrown out by the judge, as frivolous, in minutes. But there is a cost in both dollars and, my wife will confirm, despondency.

How to fight the bad guys

So shining the light of publicity on these schools can certainly do no harm, but I'm afraid that books and even articles like this may do little more than accelerate the hand-wringing.

Wouldn't it be fine if there were a consortium of legitimate universities and companies in the business of education that worked to eradicate the problem? They could do it through a combination of individual action, group action (especially media notification and advertising boycotts), and working for the passage of meaningful legislation and the enforcement of existing laws. Like the computer industry's software piracy efforts, organizations that might be fiercely competitive most of the time work together in this arena for their common good.

◆ *Individual school action.* I believe that the bigger and better schools can be a force for change—if only they would. A few years ago, a completely fake Stanford University began operating from Arkansas, even selling medical degrees by mail. I couldn't interest anyone at the real Stanford in this matter, and the fake carried on for more than a year. If the president of the real Stanford had telephoned the governor of Arkansas and the editor of *USA Today* and said, "Stop this!" might something have happened much sooner?

◆ *Advertising boycotts* (or threats thereof). Recently, on the same page in the *Economist*, there were large ads for Harvard University (quite real) and Monticello University (which the state of Kansas has accused of being fake). What if Harvard (or a group of major schools) got together and said they no longer wish to be on the same pages with the fakes?

◆ *Build a fire under the FTC.* In 1998 the Federal Trade Commission published a rule that would regulate the use of the word "accredited," limiting it to schools with recognized accreditation. The FTC has successfully dealt with the misuse of other words, from "organic" to "low-tar." Enforcing this rule would be a major blow to the fakes, who count on being able to call themselves accredited.

◆ *The "graffiti" approach.* Cities have begun winning the war on graffiti by taking immediate and decisive action: monitoring trouble spots, working with community organizations, and painting over it before the sun rises the next morning. It would not be impossibly labor-intensive to monitor ads in major publications, Web sites, and well-meaning lists compiled by people who have been fooled. The very moment a bad guy appears, instant action is taken. Action in the form of a phone call followed up with a professional and comprehensive information packet to the editor, publisher, or Internet site provider from a respectable consortium of schools would do it. Perhaps another warning letter or packet to the relevant federal, state, and local authorities as well. As it happens, the advance scouts are already out there beating the bushes searching for the bad guys, and they are doing it without pay, just for the satisfaction of the chase. Point your browser to an Internet newsgroup called alt.education.distance, and you'll find a hundred or more postings a day. There are at least 50 zealots, from Australia to Switzerland, whose antennae vibrate when some questionable institution arises. They (well, actually, we) collect information, visit nearby locations to see what's there, write reports and then, well, wring our hands a lot. Of course, the group does not speak with a common voice, but I know of no other place where there is so much useful information for someone (please) to take and run with.

◆ *Educating the public.* Legitimate schools could do this through articles, brochures, books, and public relations pieces. They could even devote a percentage of advertising, marketing, and PR budgets to this purpose, possibly through pooled efforts.

◆ *Law enforcement.* For my doctoral dissertation (in communication, earned at the legitimate Michigan State University) I studied complaining and how politicians and the media deal with complaints. I learned that the personal approach is the one that usually works, especially on an issue where the politician has little personally invested. A million letters won't change a vote on abortion or gun control, but one good letter, especially from a power-possessing individual, can get a traffic light installed, the almond import quota changed, or, quite possibly, the fake schools dealt with.

The media can be significant here, too, especially in the process of getting legislators to act. In 1983 ,Arizona was the haven for many fake schools. Then the Arizona Republic did a splendid four-day, page-one series, the first article running with the headline Diploma Mills: A Festering Sore on Arizona Education. Within months the state got and enforced some tough laws, and one by one, every phony in the state moved on to Louisiana, Hawaii, South Dakota, and other places.

If the good guys turn the power of their own credibility, credentials, contacts, and connections on the fake degree sellers, and if they do it the very instant the bad guys' ads and their Web sites appear, there is a fighting chance to recapture all of the playing field.

◇◇◇◇◇◇◇◇◇◇◇◇◇◇◇◇◇◇◇◇◇

CHAPTER SEVEN

Evaluation in the Shadowlands: When Government Approval Isn't Worth the Paper It's Forged On

by Alan Contreras

f you think government officials always tell the truth, this essay is not for you. Assuming that most of you are still reading, note that as Oregon's chief academic evaluator and fraud investigator, I have had occasion to interact with officials from many nations, with people who pretended to be such officials, with school officials who pretended to have approval from such officials, with... Well, you get the idea.

The case studies discussed below are examples from the Oregon Office of Degree Authorization (ODA) work in the past five years, but there are many other such situations. For purposes of this essay I apply the term "accreditation" rather broadly unless noted. It is used to mean the formal external evaluative process a nation employs to determine whether a college and its degree programs are equivalent to others in that nation. Note that this is not quite the same as "approval"—I will discuss the reasons for this later.

Likewise, sometimes government approval of a degree-granting entity is perfectly valid, albeit utterly useless, because the government in question is not capable of establishing and maintaining academic standards for degree-granting institutions. This is true from Mississippi to the Caribbean to Asia and Europe; useless degrees know no national boundaries and occur in all cultures.

Saint Replica: Will the Real Liberia Please Stand Up?

Certain Liberian officials apparently authorized a privately owned entity called the "National Board of Education" (NBOE) to "accredit" distance-education colleges anywhere in the world. The NBOE also owned one such entity, a diploma mill called St. Regis University. The only known address of the "Liberian" National Board of Education was in Washington, D.C. In fact, the entire operation was based in Spokane, Washington and administered by a family who has now been indicted. The NBOE offered accreditation for a fee, with no apparent evaluation process other than a nominal application. Among its many services, the NBOE offered what it claimed were verification apostilles of the kind used by jurisdictions worldwide to validate a degree. The NBOE asserted that these apostilles could be issued with a Washington, D.C. seal, which, in effect, declared the degree to be a U.S. degree, not a Liberian degree, for a fee of $1,200 per item. By comparison, a legitimate apostille issued by the Oregon Secretary of State would cost $10. Of course, a legitimate Liberian apostille would not bear a U.S. seal. The NBOE was simply a degree-laundering operation sheltering under the flag of Liberia, not an apostille service.

In order for Oregon to determine whether the NBOE would be considered a legitimate accreditor, we needed to know the following information in order to *begin* an evaluation. The same would be true in most situations, so we set forth our criteria here:

- The operators of the NBOE, including owners, board members and shareholders, and their addresses
- The actual location of NBOE's office and corporate assets
- The names and addresses of any individuals employed by the NBOE in the United States
- The process through which NBOE obtained approval from the government of Liberia to accredit colleges
- A complete list of its accredited colleges
- What the colleges did to obtain accreditation

In addition, in any specific case, we would require release of the formal application, evaluation and approval documents for the college in question.

76 | *Guide to Bogus Institutions and Documents*
Evaluation in the Shadowlands:
When Government Approval Isn't Worth the Paper It's Forged On

None of this information was available from the NBOE Web site nor was it provided by the Liberian Embassy in Washington. Mr. Abdullah Dunbar, an embassy official at the time, even composed a letter informing us that the NBOE and St. Regis were real. They weren't—what was real was Mr. Dunbar's greed and perfidy; he was later recorded by the U.S. Secret Service during a financial transaction in which he stated that, as a diplomat, he was not concerned about being arrested for taking bribes.

The relationship between the NBOE, the Liberian government and certain diploma mills was so convoluted that even Liberian officials became confused. In a letter sent to the Oregon Office of Degree Authorization (ODA) by the Liberian Embassy in the United States, Liberia's first secretary and consul stated that Liberia "will not verify the accreditation" of Adam Smith University, even though it was recently listed as an NBOE-accredited school. However, on its Web site in March 2003, Adam Smith University, a diploma mill with a long and unattractive history of peregrinating among several U.S. states and territories, stated the following: "Adam Smith University is accredited by the Ministry of Education of the Republic of Liberia." This site also stated: "Degrees are conferred from a charter issued in the United States of America by the Commonwealth of the Northern Mariana Islands or from Liberia or the British Virgin Islands if a student prefers one of these jurisdictions." Now that's educational flexibility!

In the continued presence of filiative statements from government entities in multiple international venues, it would not be unreasonable for an evaluator to assume that some formal government review relationship exists between the supposed schools and the government of Liberia. This in turn suggests that the Liberian government has no meaningful postsecondary oversight in place or that a network of its officials is freelancing, to use the most delicate term. Neither possibility lends confidence to the idea that, once a national government "approves" an accreditor or a school, other nations and employers must recognize degrees issued under such an imprimatur as inherently valid.

The moral of this story is that government officials lie. Assume that officials who say unlikely things are lying, whether or not they have been bribed (as was the case with some Liberian officials), unless you have sufficient reliable support for their statements from additional sources. This caution

Guide to Bogus Institutions and Documents
Evaluation in the Shadowlands: | 77
When Government Approval Isn't Worth the Paper It's Forged On

applies mainly in African, Caribbean and other low-income nations. It is understandable and commendable to want to treat all people and all nations equally, giving the benefit of the doubt whenever possible, but failure to recognize that bribery and corruption are common in certain nations, cultures and regions constitutes a failure of professional due diligence on the part of an evaluator. The truth is sometimes unpleasant.

Burned by Berne: Wandering Albatross Seeks Loving Home

Berne University was formerly operated out of New Hampshire and licensed to issue degrees by the nation of St. Kitts and Nevis, which will license anything. It evacuated New Hampshire one step ahead of the posse (what part of Attorney General didn't they like?) and relocated in Pennsylvania while still holding summer courses on St. Kitts. The former academic dean sued the owners in Pennsylvania courts and won.

After the U.S. Department of Education formally withdrew Berne University's status as a Title IV eligible foreign institution (in a letter stating that it was clearly not equivalent to a U.S. college and had impossibly high awards of credit), it slunk from the Caribbean sands (St. Kitts finally withdrew its accreditation in early 2006—I guess someone forgot to pay the, uh, renewal fee). Unfortunately, its wetware escaped and reemerged as "Bernelli University," which, as of this writing, has just been approved to issue degrees in Virginia.

Evaluators are having fun with its new name by speculating that if it leaves Virginia, it will reappear in Israel as Bernstein University or as Bernadotte University in Sweden. However, my colleague Erik Johansson in Sweden tells me that, although Sweden does not protect the term "university," it *does* limit use of the royal family name Bernadotte—priorities. So the Bernites may have to go elsewhere. You too can have fun playing the Berne game.

So what's the problem? What does government approval mean on St. Kitts? Historically it meant less than nothing. You may recall that St. Kitts (population about fifty thousand) is simply stuffed with colleges and medical schools and once approved a guy in Texas to issue degrees—based on your favorite TV shows—as Eastern Caribbean University. In essence, government approval there means a business license. So what does an evaluator

78 | *Guide to Bogus Institutions and Documents*
Evaluation in the Shadowlands:
When Government Approval Isn't Worth the Paper It's Forged On

do with a document stating that a college has approval of the nation of St. Kitts and Nevis? Got a cat box?

The Universitas 21 Globule:
Hopeful Hydra or Headless Horseman?

The entity called Universitas 21 Global (hereinafter referred to as U21G) began life as a spinoff of the international storefront called Universitas 21, which still owns 50 percent of it (the rest belongs to the Thomson education group). The original entity was incorporated on the Channel Islands, which are oddly exempt from both British and French postsecondary oversight laws, but otherwise not really an issue since U21G granted no degrees in its own name. It was simply a blending device for courses taken at a number of reputable universities in multiple nations.

U21G, however, obtained what seemed at first glance to be legal status as a Singaporean degree granter. The government of Singapore issued U21G some documents that appeared to allow it degree-granting status. We referred this documentation to four major evaluators of international credentials, three in the U.S. (the American Association of Collegiate Registrars and Admissions Officers [AACRAO], Educational Credential Evaluators, Inc. [ECE] of Wisconsin and Silny Associates of Florida) and our principal Australasian evaluator, HigherEd Consulting of Australia. All four concluded that U21G degree programs did not meet the requirements of Oregon law, based on their understanding of that law and the nature of Singapore's higher education structure and regulatory norms.

Oregon law requires that for an institution to be treated as a genuine degree-granter rather than a degree mill, it must have approval in its country of origin that is equivalent to U.S. accreditation (through a recognized college evaluation process) and that all of its degrees must be valid for use in its country of origin (see ORS 348.609, OAR 583-050). All four evaluators concluded that U21G had not satisfied these policies.

The principal difficulty found by all the evaluators is that U21G is not treated as a Singaporean university, public or private, by the government of Singapore in the government's own systems and documents. In effect it appears on the surface that U21G has a business license as a degree-granting

Guide to Bogus Institutions and Documents
Evaluation in the Shadowlands:
When Government Approval Isn't Worth the Paper It's Forged On | 79

entity, but not authorization to issue *Singaporean* degrees. So, what exactly is U21G? What government backs these credentials?

The Legal Fringes: How to Read Government Action and Inaction

Although Vancouver University Worldwide in British Columbia has a provincial charter to operate, the provincial private-education authority is suing to close it and Canada does not list it with UNESCO. However, Canada has no real national-level accreditation function. Vancouver University has been gliding along for many years, issuing degrees. The province has allowed this. Are its degrees legitimate?

Greenwich University on Norfolk Island (a territory of Australia) has a parliamentary charter from the island government, but Australia's own higher education quality-control authority eventually concluded that Greenwich did not meet Australian standards (coming as no surprise given the good reputation of Australian universities in general). The charter was technically overridden by a recent higher education funding act in the Australian national parliament, but remains on the books. Greenwich provided all comers with its charter and issued degrees all over the world, asserting that its island charter made it a legitimate institution. Was it a legitimate Australian institution or a shameless diploma mill? The Australian government eventually decided that it was the latter and it relocated—apparently within hours—to California, though its periscope has been detected off Hawaii, where it initially started years ago.

Monterrey Institute for Graduate Studies (MIGS) appeared at first glance to be a branch of a legitimate Mexican institution, but it granted doctorates, something the Mexican "parent" institution does not have authority to do from Mexican officials. MIGS had offices in Texas and Florida and was a Nevada corporation, yet it had not been approved to operate as a college by any of these states. It was owned in part by Sheila Danzig of Florida, known for her Internet-based unaccredited degree activities and her role as the notorious "evaluator" who approved St. Regis degrees used by Georgia teachers (before they got caught).

Oregon's inquiries to the Mexican government, presented in both English and Spanish, received no response for months. Thanks mainly to stellar quality-control efforts by David Linkletter at the Texas Coordinating Board for

80 | *Guide to Bogus Institutions and Documents*
Evaluation in the Shadowlands:
When Government Approval Isn't Worth the Paper It's Forged On

Higher Education, MIGS appears to have passed from this earth. What government had jurisdiction over its offerings? Where was it?

American Originals: The Wild West, the Seamy South

Under the terms of the state of Oregon's settlement agreement with the entity doing business as Kennedy-Western University, neither I nor any other employee of the Oregon Student Assistance Commission may refer to the operation as a "diploma mill" or "substandard institution." As a legal matter, neither the entity nor any other of the many unaccredited suppliers licensed to give out degrees by the state of Wyoming is a degree mill under Oregon law as of mid-2006. Oregon no longer uses that term to apply to any school that is issuing valid degrees legally in the state where it operates. The entity is licensed by the state to hand out degrees; therefore it is not a degree mill.

Wyoming guarantees that degrees given by the entity are valid academic credentials acceptable to the people of Wyoming. However, late-breaking news in March 2006 suggests that the Wyoming legislature may have had enough: it has passed a bill requiring that its private colleges become accredited. It is not clear yet whether this will compel a dozen entities to migrate to the degree-mill haven state of Mississippi.

Idaho handles these situations differently: if entities don't issue degrees to Idaho residents, the state pretends that they don't exist. Local entities include a swarm of naturopathy colleges, all located in one county, the most visible of which formally links itself to the nonexistent St. Luke School of Medicine that was disowned by the Liberian government (which gives you an idea of just how truly fake it must be).

Idaho also seems to have inherited Almeda U, a suspicious operation from Florida, first extruded to Georgia, which wanted no part of it. Its, uh, campus is a few blocks from the capitol building in Boise, though no one there noticed—perhaps not a surprise, since it has no faculty, classes or anything else more substantive than a mailbox with a lawyer in it. Is it issuing degrees legally from Idaho? Well, it hasn't been kicked out.

There is a certain sump effect in the Mississippi lowlands, and a pungent slurry of unaccredited degree suppliers have crept ashore on the banks of bayous in Alabama and Mississippi, apparently unnoticed by the states' genu-

Guide to Bogus Institutions and Documents
Evaluation in the Shadowlands: 81
When Government Approval Isn't Worth the Paper It's Forged On

ine universities and state regulators. The storm surge outwash from Wyoming is likely to reach Mississippi by the time this book reaches you.

Breyer State University in Alabama (featured in Clay Risen's *New Republic* story in January 2006) used to be Breyer State University in Idaho, but apparently the owner, Dominick Flarey of Ohio, wanted someplace warmer than Idaho Falls to winter. Since the entity has no relationship to a Breyer, a State or a University, it could go anywhere with lax enough laws to let it operate as a legal degree-granting entity.

Mississippi seems to have inherited all of the weevils that were spat out by Louisiana when the latter state upgraded its degree-issuance laws from non-existent to visible a few years back. The only good news is that some of these suppliers, apparently operating with full knowledge of government officials in Mississippi, chose to relocate, using the term rather loosely, in the path of Hurricane Katrina. When the local Mailboxes Etc. store went under, so did the "colleges." It isn't clear yet whether notorious bodies such as Madison U, LaCrosse U, Columbus U or American World U floated away when the incoming checks did. Since the latter is actually owned by Maxine "the Alligator" Asher, operator of a sleazy "accreditor" in Los Angeles, it can presumably swim to another mailbox if needed.

One supplier that survived was the swamp-gas apparition called Novus University, still busy issuing degrees to all comers. I must, in common charity, credit Mississippi officials as having no knowledge of the owner's history as "registrar" of Edison U of Missouri, which magically reimagined itself as Addison U (after the real Edison sued) and then Acton U while bayou shopping in the Delta. As Dan Bern (no relation to Berne University) sang in *Soul,* "the skeletons in her closet have twenty pairs of shoes to choose from." All of this is detailed in Ezell and Bear's book *Degree Mills,* apparently a banned book in Jackson. I'm afraid there is nothing remotely new about this Novus.

When Oregon asked the Mississippi Department of Justice whether Novus, Madison et al. were legal degree-granters in Mississippi, they had no answer. The civilized world has asked little of Mississippi since William Faulkner's passing, but signs of a pulse in the state legislature would be refreshing.

82 | *Guide to Bogus Institutions and Documents*
Evaluation in the Shadowlands:
When Government Approval Isn't Worth the Paper It's Forged On

Innocence Abroad: The Ross Complex

When does national government approval not matter? DeVry University, a regionally accredited U.S. college that provides a variety of mainly technical programs, announced in spring 2003 that its corporate parent, DeVry Inc., was buying the Ross University medical and veterinary schools in the Caribbean in order to improve and expand DeVry's offerings. It is not unheard of for such international acquisitions to take place, but this one was special: the Ross Veterinary School is on the Caribbean island of St. Kitts. Ross has no authorization to issue degrees anywhere in the United States.

Because meaningful academic oversight on St. Kitts is nonexistent, who exactly is responsible for academic oversight and quality at the Ross Veterinary School? It is not listed by UNESCO (not that this listing means much) and it does not appear on the international list of universities. AACRAO's International Evaluation Services has never seen its degrees. The respected Florida evaluation firm Silny Associates, which has seen its degrees, considers it only comparable to an *unaccredited* U.S. college. It apparently has only the equivalent of a business license from the government of St. Kitts (we are by now familiar with their notorious oversight standards).

Has DeVry therefore purchased an overstuffed pig in a foreign poke? Can this reputable U.S. chain school convert an expensive offshore porker that falls well below the normal accreditation radar horizon into a tax-free cash cow? Ross is not a unit of DeVry University but a freestanding unit of DeVry, Inc. Fair enough. It must therefore undergo its own evaluation, but by whom, as what?

By no one, it turns out. DeVry apparently has no plans to make Ross a U.S. accredited school. According to the U.S. Department of Education, DeVry Inc. intends to keep Ross a foreign school for Title IV purposes, a much easier approval standard at the federal level since it requires no proof of academic oversight or quality, just fiscal management and a foreign business license. It appears that DeVry does not care that the Ross Veterinary School has its "approval" from a nation whose approvals are widely considered meaningless by reputable academics.

Ross Vet will therefore become an academic version of Dr. Doolittle's Pushmepullyou, a Llama-like creature aimed in two directions at once, but worse: it will be of two species, lurching about to provide a chosen face

Guide to Bogus Institutions and Documents
Evaluation in the Shadowlands:
When Government Approval Isn't Worth the Paper It's Forged On | 83

depending on who is looking. No U.S. college or accreditor could possibly treat a school authorized by St. Kitts as having meaningful foreign approval to issue degrees—yet DeVry clearly considers this irrelevant.

The U.S. Department of Education piously cites its own rules, saying that foreign schools don't have to possess the equivalent of U.S. accreditation to be eligible for U.S. financial aid money. They just need whatever the local business license is and, if it is labeled "accreditation," well, that is good enough for the feds. So DeVry has bought a federally certified foreign college that is never required to undergo external supervision by a legitimate national college oversight body in the U.S. or in its home country. And they pay no taxes on its income stream. What a deal.

Why is national governmental approval of the Ross Veterinary School a non-factor? The answer is simple: veterinary licensing boards in almost every state allow Ross graduates to sit for licensure based on their belief that these graduates have gone through an acceptable program. In effect, the U.S. states are vetting the degrees post-facto and placing themselves in the role of college approval agent in the stead of St. Kitts.

Ross is not really a St. Kitts school—it is a U.S. school flying a foreign flag of convenience. If there is ever litigation regarding the practice of these vets, it is the state licensing boards that will be playing defense, because St. Kitts is simply a painted shell. The governments in charge of the school's future are those of the U.S. states.

This picture—a reputable U.S. school purchasing a foreign degree supplier—seems strange today, but we will see it more often. Unfortunately, the common pattern is not likely to be productive mergers between reputable providers in multiple countries, but the St. Kitts pattern: wealthy U.S. proprietary schools absorbing "approved" schools in small foreign countries, whether or not local approval means anything, and using them as one-way drainage tubes through which money can flow. The fact that the Ross Veterinary School brings with it a caravan of state agency pre-approvals makes this particular purchase function differently, but it is a rare situation that future cases are unlikely to repeat.

84 | *Guide to Bogus Institutions and Documents*
Evaluation in the Shadowlands:
When Government Approval Isn't Worth the Paper It's Forged On

Multinational Oversight Issues

Even legitimate colleges can get entangled with bogus degree suppliers. One legitimate U.S. college opened a branch campus in Israel that turned out to be in part a diploma mill. Citizens of Israel got lots of degrees (apparently some resulted from actual work and some did not), some Israeli officials became richer and more popular (for a while) and the U.S. school got a black eye. This is a very hard situation to oversee because the U.S. provider was not a diploma mill inside the U.S.; it just had poor oversight of its foreign cash cow. This is true of most cash cows: as long as the cash is flowing, the curious lack of mooing in the barn is ignored.

Another recent example comes from Singapore and, I am sorry to say, from Oregon. We were contacted by a citizen of Singapore who had "earned" a degree from an Oregon supplier. Unfortunately there is no such Oregon school, just an incorporated business (now snuffed) that has a name like a college. The incorporator, a Nevada citizen, uses the state-issued business license as proof that the "school" is government-approved and sells degrees mainly in Asia. He makes no attempt to sell these within Oregon so we did not even know of his existence.

The true core of this problem is illustrated by the Singaporean degree holder's concern. The user was troubled not because he had been scammed or because we had not done our job in catching the perpetrator, but because we insisted that the degree was illegitimate. It seems that under Singapore law this "U.S. approved degree" was legal for use and he wanted to use it. So the U.S. is not only the victim of international falsity in academic credentials, but also the architect, since some states do not prohibit the operation of diploma mills.

What to do as an Evaluator

There are several questions to ask when faced with a document from a foreign country that demonstrates doubtful conditions for college evaluation and approval or when false statements may be involved. Here are the basics:

◆ **Do evaluative and approval standards exist in the nation?** If you or your contracted foreign degree evaluator can't obtain a copy from the appropriate national government agency, assume that it doesn't exist. This is where the distinction between *accreditation* and *approval* is

Guide to Bogus Institutions and Documents
Evaluation in the Shadowlands: | 85
When Government Approval Isn't Worth the Paper It's Forged On

crucial and often forgotten. Oregon law, upon which the laws of some other states are now in part based, requires that degrees have the *foreign equivalent* of federally-recognized U.S. accreditation.

U.S. accreditation is *not* the approval to issue degrees. Accreditors do not have that power. In the U.S., approval to issue degrees comes from state governments and from nowhere else, with the exception of a few tribal colleges and institutions such as the military academies established by Congress. A foreign government's approval to issue degrees, absent a showing that the institution has been evaluated and found acceptable, cannot meet the equivalency standard. That does not mean that we need the entire universe of self-studies, visitation teams and other investigative pursuits, but it does mean that a business license by itself cannot confer equivalency.

◆ **Can the school prove that it met the standards?** Can you obtain copies of the actual application, evaluation and approval documentation from an appropriate governmental agency? If not, assume that there are none.

◆ **Are the standards sufficient?** Are you persuaded that the evaluative standards as applied to the school are adequate to ensure comparability with your school or agency requirements? This involves professional judgment and, as always in such cases, you should note clearly why you made a particular decision, in case of litigation. A notation such as "refused to identify its faculty" is very helpful, while "stinks like a dead nutria" may not carry quite as much weight.

◆ **Are the evaluative and approval documents true?** That is, can you determine using normal professional evaluative techniques that the document of approval to issue degrees is genuine and that it actually conveys that authority in the manner customary in that country? Can it be confirmed by additional sources independent of the original provider?

◆ **Are the degrees valid for use inside the country issuing the approval?** If not, a red flag the size of Nevis ought to start flapping in your mind.

86 | *Guide to Bogus Institutions and Documents*
Evaluation in the Shadowlands:
When Government Approval Isn't Worth the Paper It's Forged On

This screening point is especially effective with professional programs such as medical degrees, which are often invalid inside the nation of supposed approval (*e.g.*, if degrees from St. Christopher's College of Medicine are not valid for use to practice medicine in Senegal where it claims to hold a license, they should not be accepted as valid in your jurisdiction).

◆ **Are the degrees usable at other schools in the country of issue?** This is a helpful add-on to the general validity of use. In general the two go together, but not always, and if other universities won't accept the degrees, then the school may not be of sufficient quality, though it may be real. This is a standard that can especially be applied to the U.S., where accredited colleges generally don't accept degrees from unaccredited colleges for purposes of employment as faculty.

The problem facing those of us who try to keep bad foreign credentials out of society is that we can no longer rely on a mere government imprimatur as an indicator of legitimacy. When the government of Malawi is willing to "accredit" a U.S. diploma mill, Senegal signs off on a medical school that consists of a clinic built next to a doctor's office, and Caribbean governments allow all sorts of "schools" to operate on their islands—where do we turn for a thumb large enough to jam into this hole in the academic dike?

Determining the acceptability of degrees issued in other countries must remain firmly out of the hands of politicians local, national and international and in the hands of people to whom the validity of degrees is a genuine issue, especially in the case of colleges. No college or indeed any other employer should ever be told by its national or state government, let alone the United Nations or the World Trade Organization, that a degree from Big Al's Offshore College (whether "offshore" is St. Kitts or St. Louis) must be accepted at face value. Even my office, enforcing one of the nation's strictest degree-use laws, can only screen bad degrees out; we cannot require an employer to accept a degree.

Only in a legal environment in which doubtful degrees can be promptly investigated and, if necessary, screened out, can colleges and other employers make informed decisions as to whether a foreign degree is truly usable as a

Guide to Bogus Institutions and Documents
Evaluation in the Shadowlands: | 87
When Government Approval Isn't Worth the Paper It's Forged On

credential for a particular purpose. That is why degrees can never be treated as a commodity while no meaningful international or even national screening mechanism is available. The notion that nations are obligated to recognize the equivalence of each other's degrees is ridiculous—degrees are not bauxite or maize. That is also why each state should have laws on the books disallowing the use of unaccredited or non-equivalent foreign degrees as credentials in the absence of a genuine screening process.

It is irrational, dangerous and bad public policy to assume that all degrees issued in foreign countries are valid merely because of support by some official in that country. The evidence is quite clear that such assertions are often meaningless except as an indicator of the relative probity of officials in the country in question. Only careful, local case-by-case evaluation of foreign degrees and the exercise of uncompromised professional judgment can be accurate and successful in the current political and legal environment.

88 | *Guide to Bogus Institutions and Documents*
Evaluation in the Shadowlands:
When Government Approval Isn't Worth the Paper It's Forged On

CHAPTER EIGHT

"Legalization":
The Apostille

by LesLee Stedman

A s an education administrator, it is likely that at some point you will be asked about the "apostille." What is it? Do I need one? How can I get one? Is there a fee?

The U.S. State Department explains in its brochure on Document Authentication that documents issued in one country, which need to be used in another country, must be "authenticated" or "legalized" before they can be recognized as valid in the foreign country. This process involves placing various seals on the document. In the United States, the apostille is actually a sealed certificate that confirms the authority of a public official, such as a notary public, town clerk, or judge to act in a particular capacity in connection with a document that he or she has signed. Sometimes referred to as a "stamp" or a "gold seal," the authentication certificate will verify that the named individual and his or her position are a matter of record in the Secretary of State's Office. The certificate will only be prepared if the official has in fact executed the document properly and can only be attached to a signed original or a sealed certified copy from a public record keeper, such as a town clerk.

Background

The Convention that created the apostille-the Hague Convention Abolishing the Requirement of Legalization for Foreign Public Documents-was adopted in 1961, and although the United States ratified this Convention 20 years ago, in 1981, the concept of apostille is still foreign to many higher education administrators. To better understand how the apostille came to be, who needs it and for what purpose, and how to get it, some background information is necessary.

THE HAGUE CONFERENCE

The Hague Conference on Private International Law convened its first session in 1893 in the Netherlands. This intergovernmental organization undertook to "work for the progressive unification of the rules of private international law" (Article 1 of the Statute of the Hague Conference). To achieve this goal, the Hague Conference negotiated and drafted multilateral treaties called "Conventions."

THE 1961 CONVENTION

In 1961, the Hague Convention Abolishing the Requirement of Legalization for Foreign Public Documents (Convention #12) was concluded. This Convention dealt specifically with the process for "legalizing" or authenticating foreign public documents for use abroad. Until that time, the process had been time-consuming, costly, and complicated. Now, documents that have the special Hague Legalization Certificate are accepted in other countries where the treaty is recognized. This Legalization Certificate is known as the "apostille."

Documents recognized by the Hague Legalization Certificate include powers of attorney, affidavits, birth, death, and marriage records, incorporation papers, deeds, patent applications, home studies, and other legal papers. The number and type of authentication certificates needed depend on the nature of the document and whether or not the foreign country is a party to the multilateral treaty on "legalization" of documents. If your document is intended for use in a country which is a party to the Hague Convention Abolishing the Requirement of Legalization for Foreign Public Documents, obtaining a special apostille certificate is generally all that is required.

Annex to the Convention

Model of certificate

The certificate will be in the form of a square at least 9 centimetres long.

APOSTILLE

(Convention de La Haye du 5 octobre 1961)

1. Country:...

This public document

2. has been signed by..

....

3. acting in the capacity of...

4. bears the seal/stamp of..

....

Certified

5. at... 6. the.....................................

7. by...

8. №..

9. Seal/stamp: 10. Signature:

....

However, if the country where the document will be used has not signed and ratified the Convention, you will have to begin the cumbersome, time-consuming process of obtaining a series of certifications known as the "chain authentication method." This procedure requires multiple seals to be placed on documents, verification by individuals and bureaus at various levels of government, as well payment of numerous fees. It is literally a paper chase in which authorities will have to attest to the validity of a succession of seals beginning with your document and ending with the seal of the foreign embassy or consulate in the United States. Hague Convention #12 simplified this procedure for member nations by eliminating many links in the "chain."

The following components will appear on the apostille:

◆ Name of country from which the document emanates

◆ The capacity in which the person signing the document has acted

◆ In the case of unsigned documents, the name of the authority which has affixed the seal or stamp

◆ Place of certification

◆ Date of certification

◆ The authority issuing the certificate

◆ Number of certificate

◆ Seal or stamp of authority issuing certificate

◆ Signature of authority issuing certificate

In 1981, the United States joined the ranks of many other nations that had already signed and ratified this Convention. Table 1 lists the countries and territories adhering to the 1961 Convention. Within and between these countries, documents bearing the apostille are entitled to recognition without further authentication.

Table 1. Countries Adhering to the 1961 Convention	
Countries that have signed and ratified the Convention (applicability formally confirmed)	Countries, now independent, that previously signed and ratified the Convention (no formal confirmation of continued applicability of Convention received)
Andorra, Anguilla, Antigua and Barbuda, Argentina, Armenia, Aruba, Australia, Austria, Bahamas, Barbados, Belarus, Belgium, Belize, Bermuda, Bosnia-Herzegovina, Botswana, British Antarctic Territory, British Virgin Islands, Brunei, Bulgaria, Cayman Islands, Croatia, Cyprus, El Salvador, Falkland Islands, Fiji, Finland, France, French Guyana, French Polynesia, Guadeloupe, Germany, Gibraltar, Greece, Guernsey (Bailiwick of), Hong Kong, Hungary, Isle of Man, Israel, Italy, Japan, Jersey (Bailiwick of), Latvia, Lesotho, Liechtenstein, Luxembourg, Macao, Macedonia, Malawi, Malta, Marshall Islands, Martinique, Mauritius, Mexico, Montserrat, Netherlands, Netherlands Antilles (Curacao, Bonaire, St. Martin, St. Eustatius and Saba), New Caledonia, Norway, Panama, Portugal, Reunion, Russian Federation, St. Christopher (Kitts) and Nevis, St. Georgia and South Sandwich Islands, St. Helena, St. Lucia, St. Pierre and Miquelon, St. Vincent and The Grenadines, San Marino, Seychelles, Slovenia, South Africa, Spain, Suriname, Swaziland, Switzerland, Tonga, Turkey, Turks and Caicos, United Kingdom, United States, Wallis and Futuna	Angola, Comoros Islands (Formerly Moroni), Djibouti (formerly Affars and Issas), Dominica, Grenada, Kiribati (formerly Gilbert Islands), Mozambique, Solomon Islands (formerly British Solomon Islands), Tuvalu (formerly Ellice Islands), Vanuatu (formerly New Hebrides)

ACADEMIC DOCUMENTS

In 1983, the Department of State and u.s. embassies and consulates abroad ceased authenticating or providing true certified copies of academic transcripts, credentials, and degrees. For those individuals wanting to enroll in primary, secondary, or postsecondary schooling in the u.s., it was decided that if they completed all or part of their education overseas, requiring such documents who was unnecessary. The Immigration and Naturalization Service (ins), likewise, determined that "legalization" of foreign academic credentials is not generally necessary for u.s. immigration purposes. However, there will be instances when foreign nationals who have been educated in the United States wish to have their academic records authenticated for use abroad. The following step-by-step process can also be found on the State Department's Web site at www.state.gov/m/a/auth/. (Detailed information about legalizing documents for use in countries that do not abide by the 1961 Hague Convention Abolishing the Requirement of Legalization for Foreign Public Documents is also located at this site.)

Colleges, Universities, and Other Postsecondary Institutions

Hague Legalization Convention Country Method (for use in countries that have adopted the 1961 Hague Convention Abolishing the Requirement of Legalization for Foreign Public Documents):

1. Obtain from the registrar of the university an official true copy of the credentials, a statement attesting to the accuracy of the credentials, executed by the registrar, and have the statement notarized before a notary public in the registrar's office, business office, or elsewhere in the university.
2. Take the document to the clerk of the court of the country wherein the notary was licensed or commissioned, to obtain a notarial certificate suitable for use abroad.
3. Send the document to the competent authority in the u.s. for the Hague Legalization Convention (usually the state Secretary of State) for the apostille certificate.

Primary and Secondary Schools

Hague Legalization Convention Country Method (for use in countries that have adopted the 1961 Hague Convention Abolishing the Requirement of Legalization for Foreign Public Documents):

1. Obtain a transcript from the school which bears the seal of the school and the signature of the principal.

- Ask the school to send the transcript to the County Board of Education, Superintendent of Schools or other official body which can authenticate the school's seal with a superior seal. Ask that authority to send the document to the state Secretary of State's office.
- Obtain authentication of the transcript from the state Secretary of State's office (www.state.gov/m/a/auth/).

WHERE DOES ONE GET THE APOSTILLE?

In the u.s., competent authorities for affixing the apostille vary from state to state. Table 2 provides not only contact information by United States state and territory, but fee information as well.

Sources
Hague Conference On Private International Law: www.hcch.net/
U.S. State Department Office of Authentication: www.state.gov/m/a/auth/
American Embassy in Spain: www.embusa.es
U.S. Department of State, Bureau of Consular Affairs, Overseas Citizens Services: http://travel.state.gov/law/legal/treaty/treaty-783.html
Office of the Secretary of the State of Connecticut: www.sots.ct.gov

Table 2. Access to the Apostille (by State)					
ST	**Contact Address**	**Internet**	**Telephone**	**Designated Authority**	**Fee**
AK	Office of the Lieutenant Governor Authentications Department 240 Main Street, Suite 300 Juneau, Alaska 99801	http://ltgov.gov. state.ak.us/notary/ authentications.php	(907) 465-3509	Lieutenant Governor; Attorney General; Clerk of the Supreme Court	$2.00
AL	Secretary of State Document Authentication 11 S. Union St., Suite 208 Montgomery, AL 36104	www.sos.state.al.us/ authenticate/index.htm	(334) 242-7224	Secretary of State	$5.00
AR	Office of Secretary of State Corporations Division State Capitol Little Rock, AR 72201-1094	www.sos.arkansas.gov/ elections/elections_pdfs/ authentication.pdf	(501) 682-3409	Secretary of State; Chief Deputy Secretary of State	$10.00
AS	Office of the Governor Executive Office Building Third Floor, Utulei Pago Pago, AS 96799		011-684- 633-4116	Secretary of American Samoa; Attorney General of American Samoa	

ST	Contact Address	Internet	Telephone	Designated Authority	Fee
AZ	Arizona Secretary of State Attn: Notary Department 1700 W. Washington, 7th Fl. Phoenix, AZ 85007	www.azsos.gov/ business_services/ notary/notaryqanda. htm#23/	(602) 542-4758	Secretary of State; Assistant Secretary of State	$3.00
CA	Office of the Secretary of State Notary Public Section 1500 11th Street 2nd Floor Sacramento, CA 95814 (walk-up) P.O. Box 942877 Sacramento, CA 94277-0001 (mailing)	www.ss.ca.gov/ business/notary/notary_ authentication.htm	(916) 653-3595	Secretary of State; any Assistant Secretary of State; any Deputy Secretary of State	$20.00
CO	Office of the Secretary of State Licensing Division (nota- rized documents) Elections Division (docu- ments of public record) 1700 Broadway, Suite 300 Denver, CO 80290	www.sos.state.co.us/ pubs/bingo_raffles/ apostille.htm	(303) 894-2200 x6409 (notarized documents) (303) 894- 2200 x6307 (documents of public record)	Secretary of State; Deputy Secretary of State	None for notarized docu- ments; $2.00 for copies of documents of public record
CT	Commercial Recording Division Connecticut Secretary of State 30 Trinity St. Hartford, CT 06106	www.sots.ct.gov/ CommercialRecording/ CRDAuthApos/ EnglishAuthOrdForm.pdf	(860) 509-6002	Secretary of State; Deputy Secretary of State	$20.00
DC	Office of the Secretary, D.C. Notary Commissions & Authentications Section 441-4th Street, N.W. (One Judiciary Square) Washington, D.C. 20001		(202) 727-3117	Executive Secretary; Assistant Executive Secretary; Mayor's Special Assistant and Assistant to the Executive Secretary; Secretary of the District of Columbia	$10.00
DE	Division of Corporations John G. Townsend Bldg. 401 Federal Street, Suite 4 Dover, DE 19901	www.state.de.us/ sos/faqs.shtml	(302) 739-3073	Secretary of State; Acting Secretary of State	$20.00
FL	Department of State Tallahassee Office Clifton Building 2661 Executive Center Circle Tallahassee, FL 32301	http://notaries.dos.state. fl.us/notproc7.html	(850) 245-6945	Secretary of State	$20.00

Table 2. Access to the Apostille (by State)

Table 2. Access to the Apostille (by State)

ST	Contact Address	Internet	Telephone	Designated Authority	Fee
GA	Georgia Superior Court Clerks' Cooperative Authority Notary Division 1875 Century Blvd., Suite 100 Atlanta, GA 30345	www.gsccca.org/Projects/apost.asp	(404) 327-6023 (800) 304-5175	Georgia Superior Court Clerks' Cooperative Authority	$3.00
GU	Office of the Governor P.O. Box 2950 Agana, GU 96910		011-671-472-1537	Director, Department of Administration; Acting Director, Department of Administration; Deputy Director, Department of Administration; Acting Deputy Director, Department of Administration	
HI	Office of the Lieutenant Governor State Capitol, 5th Floor Honolulu, HI 96813	www.hawaii.gov/ltgov/office/apostilles/	(808) 586-0255	Lieutenant Governor of the State of Hawaii	$1.00
IA	Office of Secretary of State Lucas Building 321 E. 12th St. Des Moines, IA 50319		(515) 281-5204	Secretary of State; Deputy Secretary of State	$5.00
ID	Office of Secretary of State Notary Department Box 83720 Boise, ID 83720	www.idsos.state.id.us/notary/apostill.htm	(208) 332-2810	Secretary of State; Chief Deputy Secretary of State; Deputy Secretary of State; Notary Public Clerk	$10.00
IL	Office of the Secretary of State Index Department Notaries Public Division 111 E. Monroe St. Springfield, IL 62756	www.sos.state.il.us/departments/index/division.html	(217) 782-7017	Secretary of State; Assistant Secretary of State; Deputy Secretary of State	$2.00
IN	Indiana Secretary of State Authentication Department 302 W. Washington Street, Room E-018 Indianapolis, IN 46204	www.in.gov/sos/business/apostille/	(317) 232-2677	Secretary of State; Deputy Secretary of State	None

Table 2. Access to the Apostille (by State)

ST	Contact Address	Internet	Telephone	Designated Authority	Fee
KS	Office of Secretary of State State Capitol, Second Floor Topeka, KS 66612		(913) 296-2744	Secretary of State; Assistant Secretary of State; any Deputy Assistant Secretary of State	$5.00
KY	Office of Secretary of State Apostilles Branch Capitol Building 700 Capital Ave., Suite 156 Frankfort, KY 40601	http://sos.ky.gov/ adminservices/ apostilles.htm	(502) 564-7330	Secretary of State; Assistant Secretary of State	$5.00
LA	Louisiana Secretary of State Commissions Division P.O. Box 94125 Baton Rouge, LA 70804-9125	www.sos.louisiana. gov/elections/ commis/commis-index. htm#apostille	(225) 922-0330	Secretary of State	$20.00
MA	Secretary of the Commonwealth Public Records Division Commissions Section McCormack Bldg., Room 1719 One Ashburton Place Boston, MA 02108	www.sec.state.ma.us/ pre/precom/comidx.htm	(617) 727-2832		$6.00
MD	Office of Secretary of State 16 Francis Street, Jeffrey Building, 1st Floor Annapolis MD 21401	www.sos.state. md.us/Certifications/ faq.htm#apos	(410) 974-5521	Secretary of State	$5.00
ME	Office of Secretary of State Bureau of Corporations, Elections and Commissions 101State House Station Augusta, ME 04333	www.maine.gov/ sos/cec/notary/ apostilles.html	(207) 624-7736	Secretary of State; Deputy Secretary of State	$10.00
MI	Department of State Office of the Great Seal 108 South Washington Square, Suite 1 Lansing, MI 48918-1750 (walk-in) or Detroit New Center Super!Center Cadillac Place Building 3046 West Grand Boulevard, Suite L650 Detroit, MI (walk-in) or Michigan Department of State Office of the Great Seal 7064 Crowner Drive Lansing, MI 48918 (mail)	www.michigan. gov/sos/1,1607,7-127-1638_8734—-,00.html	(517) 373-2531	Secretary of State; Deputy Secretary of State	$1.00

ST	Contact Address	Internet	Telephone	Designated Authority	Fee
				Table 2. Access to the Apostille (by State)	
MN	Office of Secretary of State 180 State Office Bldg. St. Paul, MN 55155	www.sos.state. mn.us/home/index. asp?page=12&select_ faq_by_faq_cat=8	(651) 296-2803	Secretary of State; Deputy Secretary of State	$5.00
MO	Office of Secretary of State Commissions 600 West Main, Room 322 Jefferson City, MO 65101	www.sos.mo.gov/ business/commissions/ certify.asp	(314) 751-2783 (800) 223-6535	Secretary of State; Deputy Secretary of State	$10.00
MP				Attorney General; Acting Attorney General; Clerk of the Court, Commonwealth Trial Court; Deputy Clerk, Commonwealth Trial Court	
MS	Office of Secretary of State P.O. Box 136 Jackson, MS 39205-0136		(601) 359-1615	Secretary of State; any Assistant Secretary of State	$5.00
MT	Office of Secretary of State Notary/Certification Section P.O. Box 202801 Helena, MT 59620-2801	http://sos.state.mt.us/ Notary/Certifications.asp	(406) 444-1877	Secretary of State; Chief Deputy Secretary of State; Government Affairs Bureau Chief	$10.00
NC	Office of Secretary of State Authentication Division 2 South Salisbury St. Raleigh, NC 27601-2903 (walk-in) or Document Authentication Office Office of Secretary of State P.O. Box 29622 Raleigh, NC 27626-0622 (mail)	www.secretary. state.nc.us/authen/ AuthFAQ.aspx	(919) 807-2140	Secretary of State; Deputy Secretary of State	$10.00
ND	Office of Secretary of State Capitol Building Bismarck, ND 58505		(701) 328-2900	Secretary of State; Deputy Secretary of State	$10.00

Table 2. Access to the Apostille (by State)

ST	Contact Address	Internet	Telephone	Designated Authority	Fee
NE	Nebraska Secretary of State Notary Division State Capitol Bldg., Rm. 1301 1445 K St. Lincoln, NE 68508 (walk-in) or Nebraska Secretary of State Notary Division Box 95104 Lincoln, NE 68509 (mail)	www.sos.state.ne.us/ business/notary/ not_auth.html	(402) 471-2558	Secretary of State; Deputy Secretary of State	$10.00
NH	Office of Secretary of State Statehouse, Room 204 Concord, NH 03301 (walk-in) Office of Secretary of State 107 North Main St. Concord, NH 03301 (mail)	www.sos.nh.gov/ certific.htm	(603) 271-3242	Secretary of State; Deputy Secretary of State	$10.00
NJ	New Jersey Division of Revenue Notary Unit PO Box 452 Trenton, NJ 08646	www.state.nj.us/ treasury/revenue/dcr/ programs/apostilles.htm	(609) 292-9292	Secretary of State; Assistant Secretary of State	$25.00
NM	Office of Secretary of State Operations Division 325 Don Gaspar, Suite 300 Santa Fe, NM 87503	www.sos.state.nm.us/ Main/Operations/ Appost-Cert.htm	(800) 477-3632	Secretary of State	$3.00
NY	Upstate Counties: Miscellaneous Records 162 Washington Ave. Albany, NY 12231 Downstate Counties: Department of State Certification Unit 123 William Street, 19th Floor New York, NY 10038	www.dos.state.ny.us/ corp/msrfaq.html	(518) 474-8642 (212) 417-5684	Secretary of State; Executive Deputy Secretary of State; any Deputy Secretary of State; any Special Deputy Secretary of State	$10.00 $10.00
NV	Office of Secretary of State 101 N. Carson St. Carson City, NV 89701	http://sos.state.nv.us/ notary/apostille.htm	(702) 684-5708	Secretary of State; Chief Deputy Secretary of State; Deputy Secretary of State	$20.00

Table 2. Access to the Apostille (by State)

ST	Contact Address	Internet	Telephone	Designated Authority	Fee
OH	Ohio Secretary of State Elections Division Borden Building 180 E. Broad St., 15th fl. Columbus, OH 43215 (walk-in) or Office of Secretary of State Elections Division P.O. Box 2828 Columbus, OH 43216 (mail)	www.sos.state.oh.us/ sos/ElectionsVoter/ documentAuthen. aspx?Section=22	(614) 466-2585	Secretary of State; Assistant Secretary of State	$5.00
OK	Office of Secretary of State 2300 N. Lincoln Blvd. Suite 101 Oklahoma City, OK 73105		(405) 521-4211	Secretary of State; Assistant Secretary of State; Budget Officer of the Secretary of State	$25.00
OR	Office of Secretary of State Corporation Division Notary Public Section 255 Capitol St. NE Suite 151 Salem, OR 97310	www.filinginoregon. com/notary/ authentication.htm	(503) 986-2593	Secretary of State; Deputy Secretary of State; Acting Secretary of State; Assistant to the Secretary of State	$10.00
PA	Department of State Bureau of Commissions, Elections and Legislation Rm. 210, N. Office Bldg. Harrisburg, PA 17120	www.dos.state. pa.us/bcel/cwp/view. asp?A=1099&QUESTION_ ID=431658	(717) 787-5280	Secretary of the Commonwealth; Any Deputy Secretary of the Commonwealth, Commissioner of the Bureau of Commissions, Elections and Legislation	$15.00
PR	Office of the Secretary of State Department of State Box 3271 San Juan, PR 00902-3271		(809) 723-4334	Under Secretary of State; Assistant Secretary of State for External Affairs; Assistant Secretary of State; Chief, Certifications Office; Director, Office of Protocol	

ST	Contact Address	Internet	Telephone	Designated Authority	Fee
		Table 2. Access to the Apostille (by State)			
RI	Office of Secretary of State Corporations Division Notary Public Section 148 W. River Street Providence, RI 02904-2615	www.sec.state. ri.us/corps/apostille/ authen.html	(401) 222-3040	Secretary of State; First Deputy Secretary of State; Second Deputy Secretary of State	$5.00
SC	Office of Secretary of State Notary Division P.O. Box 11350 Columbia, SC 29211	www.scsos.com/ notariesbc.htm	(803) 734-2512	Secretary of State	$2.00
SD	Office of Secretary of State 500 E. Capitol Ave. Suite 204 Pierre, SD 57501-5070	www.sdsos.gov/ adminservices/ apostilles.shtm	(605) 773-3537	Secretary of State; Deputy Secretary of State	$5.00
TN	Department of State Division of Business Services Notary Commissions Unit William R. Snodgrass Tower, 6th Floor 312 Eighth Ave. N. Nashville, TN 37243	http://tennessee.gov/ sos/forms/apos.pdf	(615) 741-3699	Secretary of State	$2.00
TX	Texas Secretary of State Notary Public Unit 1019 Brazos, Rm. 214 Austin, TX (walk-in) Texas Secretary of State Notary Public Unit P.O. Box 13375 Austin, TX 78711 (mail)	http://txsos-7.sos.state. tx.us/authfaqs.shtml	(512) 463-5705	Secretary of State; Assistant Secretary of State	$15.00
UT	Office of the Lieutenant Governor Authentication Office State Capitol Complex East Building, Suite E-325 P.O. Box 140760 Salt Lake City, UT 84114-0760	http://governor. state.ut.us/lt_gover/ apostilletemplate.html	(801) 538-1041	Lieutenant Governor; Deputy Lieutenant Governor; Administrative Assistant	$10.00
VA	Office of Secretary of Commonwealth Authentications Division 1111 East Broad St. 4th Floor Richmond, Virginia 23219	www.commonwealth. virginia.gov/ OfficialDocuments/ authentications.cfm	(804) 786-2441	Secretary of the Commonwealth; Chief Clerk, Office of the Secretary of Commonwealth	$10.00

Table 2. Access to the Apostille (by State)

ST	Contact Address	Internet	Telephone	Designated Authority	Fee
VI	Office of the Lieutenant Governor 7 & 8 King St. Christiansted, St. Croix USVI 00802		(809) 774-2991	No authority designated; refer requests to the U.S. Department of State, Authentications Office, 2400 M St. N.W., Washington, D.C. 20520, (202) 647-5002	
VT	Office of Secretary of State 26 Terrace St. Montpelier, VT 05609-1103	http://vermont-archives.org/notary/authentication.html	(802) 828-2308	Secretary of State; Deputy Secretary of State	$2.00
WA	Secretary of State Corporations Division Apostille and Certificate Program 801 Capitol Way South Olympia, WA 98504-0228 (walk-in) or Secretary of State Apostille and Certificate Program PO Box 40228 Olympia, WA 98504-0228 (mail)	www.secstate.wa.gov/apostilles/	(360) 586-2268 or (360) 586-7524	Secretary of State; Assistant Secretary of State; Director, Department of Licensing	$15.00
WI	Office of Secretary of State Certification Desk P.O. Box 7848 Madison, WI 53707-7848	www.sos.state.wi.us/apostilles.htm	(608) 266-5503	Secretary of State; Assistant Secretary of State	$10.00
WY	Office of Secretary of State The Capitol Building 200 West 24th St. Cheyenne, WY 82002-0020	http://soswy.state.wy.us/authenti/authenti.htm	(307) 777-5860	Secretary of State; Deputy Secretary of State	$3.00
WV	Office of Secretary of State 1900 Kanawha Blvd. E. Building 1, No. 157-K Charleston, WV 25305-0770	www.wvsos.com/execrecords/other/authentication.htm	(304) 558-6000	Secretary of State; Under Secretary of State; any Deputy Secretary of State	$10.00

CHAPTER NINE

∞∞∞∞∞∞∞∞∞∞∞∞∞∞∞

Accreditation Mills

by Allen Ezell

I n the Winter 2002 issue of *C&U* (Volume 77, No. 3), I authored the article, "Diploma Mills—Past, Present, and Future." In this article, a diploma mill was defined as "an organization that awards degrees without requiring students to meet educational standards for such degrees; it either receives fees from its so-called students on the basis of fraudulent misrepresentation, or it makes it possible for the recipients of its degrees to perpetrate a fraud on the public."

Diploma mills (degree mills) do not operate in a vacuum. To buttress their alleged legitimacy, they require support from:

◆ purported independent academic referral entities
◆ accreditation mills
◆ transcript and records storage facilities
◆ graduate verification entities
◆ credential evaluation companies.

Dr. Judith Eaton, president, Council for Higher Education Accreditation (CHEA), described the negative impact of diploma mills. "Degree mills are a disservice to society. They undermine confidence in higher education. They undermine confidence in credentials." The same can be reiterated for accreditation mills, but more importantly, it should be noted that they devalue the entire legitimate accreditation process. Degree mills and accreditation mills cast a shadow on higher education. (For more information, see CHEA Fact Sheet #6, "Important Questions About 'Diploma Mills' and 'Accreditation Mills,'" available at www.chea.org/pdf/fact_sheet_6_diploma_mills.pdf).

Accreditation

Accreditation is defined by Merriam-Webster Online Dictionary as "to give official authorization to or approval of; to provide with credentials; to recognize or vouch for as conforming with a standard; to recognize (as an educational institution) as maintaining standards that qualify the graduates for admission to higher or more specialized institutions or for professional practice; to consider or recognize as outstanding." Others simply define accreditation as "the act of granting credit or recognition, especially with regard to an educational institution that maintains suitable standards."

According to CollegeDegreeGuide.com, accreditation has two basic fundamental purposes:

◆ to assure the quality of the institution or program, and
◆ to assist in the improvement of the institution or program.

Accreditation also establishes a benchmark, which then eases the transition or move from one accredited school to another, and the acceptance of academic records from each. It also provides a legitimate base for graduates to enter the workforce. Accreditation does not, however, provide automatic acceptance by an institution of credit earned at another institution, nor does it give assurance that employers will accept graduates. It is always the responsibility of the receiving institution or employer to verify the applicant's credentials.

The United States government does not accredit colleges, unlike many foreign countries. Similarly, the federal government does not accredit or conduct academic evaluation of foreign colleges. Generally, this is left to the discretion of the respective Ministries of Education or other appropriate bodies. The United States Department of Education (DOE) recognizes eight regional, eleven national, and 66 specialized and professional accrediting organizations. For a complete listing, visit www.ed.gov/admins/finaid/accred/index.html.

Accreditation Mills

No standard definition of an accreditation mill exists. However, I believe it can be defined as:

An organization—not recognized by the U.S. Department of Education, nor by the Council for Higher Education Accreditation—that grants "accreditation" without requiring the purported college or university to meet generally accepted standards for such "accreditation." It has no concern over the quality of instruction, nor with improvement at the entity which it "accredits." It either receives fees from its so-called "accredited" institutions on the basis of fraudulent misrepresentations, or it makes it possible for the purported college or university receiving such "accreditation" (or its "graduates") to perpetrate a fraud on the public.

Further, an accreditation mill:

- is a purported accrediting entity that is not recognized by the U.S. Department of Education, CHEA, nor by any recognized regional or specialized accrediting association.
- has no official recognition, and cannot impart the same on others.
- offers "accreditation status" to institutions in a short amount of time.
- offers permanent or lifetime accreditation status without requirement for subsequent reviews.
- has few, or any of its standards for accreditation published.
- has no rigid standards relating to academics or staff (also has no procedures in place to measure the level of quality of instruction to ensure that it is maintained at a level acceptable to the body that issues the degree granting right).
- sometimes "accredits" schools without their knowledge (in an effort to give itself credibility).
- does not perform onsite inspections prior to (or after) it "accredits" a school.
- only communicates by mail and telephone.
- does not operate at "arm's length" to the institutions it "accredits."
- frequently makes false statements regarding its address, ownership, staff, length of time in business, and schools that it "accredits," recognizes, and with which it is associated.

- sells its worthless "accreditation" for a flat up-front fee, with a stated amount for renewals.
- sometimes uses addresses in Washington, D.C., in an effort to imply a government affiliation or national image.
- may even select a name for itself that is similar to other legitimate entities, such as: The International Distance Education and Training Council (IDETC) vs. The Distance and Education Training Council (DETC) [legitimate entity].
- misleads or defrauds "graduates" of institutions that it "accredits."
- by engaging in all the above, makes it possible for "graduates" of institutions it "accredits" to defraud third parties, and others who rely on the degree/transcript/accreditation process.

As stated earlier, the fundamental purposes of legitimate accreditation are to assure the quality of the institution or program, and to assist in the improvement of the institution or program. Accreditation mills, on the other hand, are certainly not concerned with either of these goals. Accreditation mills are not interested in quality, institutions, or programs. The sole purpose of an accreditation mill is to help sell the wares of the degree mill. An accreditation mill is strictly a marketing tool used by a degree mill. This is part of their deception and camouflage, all designed to hide the true worthlessness of the school.

Degree mill operators know that the legitimate accreditation process is lengthy, expensive, and detailed, and that it involves a comparison of a school's curriculum, faculty, and administrative practices against strict standards. They fully realize their entity will never obtain legitimate accreditation by a recognized accrediting entity, and thus they subvert the accreditation process, by either creating their own accrediting entity or obtaining accreditation from an unrecognized entity, which may have low or no standards.

For example, Bircham University (www.bircham.edu) depicts the logos of seventeen different entities on its 'recognition and affiliations' page. Six of these "accredit" distance learning institutions. I thought having one "accreditor" was enough for a school; it is interesting to think how many people will fall victim to this display.

In a recent article by Jane Knight, University of Toronto, she states that the problem of accreditation mills is all the more confusing to potential students in this age of cross-border accreditation providers. In her article, "International Race for Accreditation Stars in Cross-Border Education," she notes that education is becoming "stateless." The challenge is to distinguish between the bona fide (those we know we can trust), and the rogue accreditors. (This article is available at www.bc.edu/bc_org/avp/soe/cihe/newsletter/ihe_pdf/ihe40.pdf.)

Our export of degree mills and accreditation mills casts doubt on the reliability of legitimate degrees conferred in the United States and of accreditation itself. Students outside the United States are particularly vulnerable since they have limited access to information. The "American" approach may be especially confusing to a student in a country where a Ministry of Education prevails. To students outside of the U.S., the mere fact that the school and accrediting entity are "American" may be the most significant reason to accept them as genuine. Coupled with the "right" name or address, a student can be convinced of their legitimacy.

Examples

Both degree mills and accreditation mills use Washington, D.C. addresses to add perceived "legitimacy" to their entities. The University of Berkley, formerly of Berkley, Michigan (now operated from a garage in Erie, Pennsylvania) uses a telephone answering service near Chicago, and touts a large number of school teachers and school district administrators, along with numerous military personnel, among its graduates. University of Berkley sells "honorary degrees" via its Web site, "University of Berkley Online." University of Berkley is "accredited" by NAPFEW (New Millennium Accrediting Partnership for Educators Worldwide), 2020 Pennsylvania Avenue, N.W., #750, Washington, D.C. 20006. On July 8, 2005, the Attorney General of Pennsylvania filed suit against Dennis J. Globosky, dba The University of Berkley, indicating that when Globosky rented the above Washington, D.C. mail drop address for NAPFEW, he indicated this acronym stood for "National Association of Police, Firefighters and Emergency Workers."

Another example is Americus University, located at 611 Pennsylvania Avenue, SE, Washington, D.C. [this is actually the address of a UPS Store].

Items to Be Aware—and Wary—of Regarding Degree Mills And Accreditation

► Accreditation is claimed from a fake or unrecognized agency.
► The fake or unrecognized accreditor also accredits legitimate schools.
► The accreditor offers a confirming telephone service or hotline for reassurance.
► As a global or international university, they don't need government approval.
► Explaining at length why accreditation is not important.*
► Claiming that Harvard and Oxford aren't accredited either.
► Accreditation claimed from a place where the word is used differently.
► Claiming accreditation is impossible because of church-state separation.
► Approval or accreditation from a fake or unrecognized country.
► Fake accreditation claimed from a real country or national agency.
► The right to confer degrees comes from wording in their articles of incorporation.

* Some of these mills state institutional accreditation is unnecessary, since they are in fact "accredited" by the good deeds of their graduates.

It claims to be "accredited" by the International Distance Learning Council (address was unknown, but it shared a telephone number with Americus University). Americus University even advertised that degrees could be obtained in 20 days. Why do you think Americus University selected a Washington, D.C. address, with a name similar to a legitimate, accredited university, with name recognition, (American University) in the same city?

On September 11, 2003, American University sued Americus University for adopting the American University design mark on their Web site, having diplomas similar in design, and using a domain name that was "confusingly similar." On October 30, 2003, the National Arbitration Forum panel ruled that the respondent registered and used the domain name www.americusuniversity.com in bad faith, and the domain name was ordered to be transferred from the respondent to the complainant. Although American University prevailed in this litigation, Americus University had operated from June 8, 2001 until October 30, 2003. Who knows how many degrees and transcripts were issued in that period. Those fake degrees and transcripts will continue to surface for years.

We have seen the use of Washington, D.C. addresses to denote government affiliation in many education frauds, including both degree mills, accreditation mills, along with academic records storage entities. Everyone wants a Washington, D.C. address and postmark to add support to their criminal enterprise.

Magnitude of the Problem

In our recently published book, *Degree Mills: The Billion Dollar Industry That Has Sold Over a Million Fake Diplomas*, Dr. John Bear and I list over 200 fake, unrecognized, and dubious accreditation agencies. Table 1 (on the following page) lists some of the more egregious accreditation mills we most often encounter (and some of the schools they "accredit").

When taking a close look at the names used by these accreditation mills, the use of the words American, Association, Council, Distance, International, National, United States, World, and Worldwide are designed to convey a broad-based image of legitimacy for their entity, if not government affiliation, and a national or international character to their mill. This deception is by design.

Government Action

Since 2003, numerous agencies and departments of the United States government have stepped up measures for legitimacy after it was found out that a Department of Homeland Security employee had obtained employment with fraudulent credentials. As a result, the Senate and House of Representatives held hearings in 2004. On January 27, 2005, due to the exposure on Capitol Hill and the General Accounting Office (GAO) citing numerous federal employees with degrees from degree mills (or from schools with unrecognized accreditation [accreditation mills]), the Office of Personnel Management (OPM) took action.

OPM has now established further educational requirements for those seeking employment with the federal government. OPM stated, "Bogus degrees from so-called degree mills ["unregulated institutions of higher education, granting degrees with few or no academic requirements"] may not be used to qualify for federal jobs or salaries. The American people expect their public servants to be honest and forthcoming." Now, only degrees accredited by an accrediting body recognized by the Secretary of the U.S. Department of Education will be accepted.

Additionally, on February 3, 2005, the Federal Trade Commission (FTC) issued a consumer alert titled, "Degree Mills: Degrees of Deception," in which they discussed accreditation mills—accreditation from a bogus, but official-sounding agency created by the degree mill. They also mentioned the basic six warning signs of degree mills (no studies/exams; no attendance; flat fee; no waiting; click here to order now, and advertising through spam or pop-ups). The FTC also issued a publication for employers titled "Avoid Fake-Degree Burns by Researching Academic Credentials." (If all businesses would take the time to verify all presented credentials up front, think of the problems and embarrassment that could later be avoided. This would go a long way to dry up the market for fraudulent credentials.)

State Laws

Each state has its own laws governing private, postsecondary education. States like Oregon, Michigan, and New Jersey lead the way in establishing standards and enforcement. There may be some light at the end of the tunnel regarding state legislation outlawing degree mills and accreditation mills.

WYOMING

Wyoming recently had a chance to create some tough laws in this arena, however, these failed to pass. Thus, Wyoming will continue to be the home base for many degree mills and also the home for several academic records storage/verification businesses.

MAINE

The state of Maine now has proposed legislation (Sec.1. 20-A MRSA Chapter 410—"False Academic Degrees or Certificates"), which defines accreditation, accreditation mill, diploma mill, degree mill, duly authorized institution of higher learning, false academic degree, and substandard school or institution of higher education. Further, Section 10802 states,

> This bill makes it illegal to issue, manufacture, and use false academic degrees or certificates to obtain employment, to obtain promotion or higher compensation in employment, to obtain admission to an institution of higher learning or in connection with any business, trade, profession or occupation. This bill also authorizes the Department of Education to protect consumers by providing Internet site information naming and updating known own state, national and international diploma mills, degree mills, accreditation mills and substandard schools.

Proposed amendments to the Texas Education Code, Section 61.302, have just been sent to the Governor of Texas (to be effective September 1, 2005), outlawing "fraudulent, substandard, or fictitious" degrees; and issuance or use of a degree from an institution that is not accredited by a recognized accrediting agency. This statute prohibits the use of such degrees to obtain employment, or obtain license or certificate to practice a trade or profession or occupation, for promotion, compensation, admission to an educational program, or gain a position in government.

This proposed new legislation may be partially the result of the recent revelations that officials of Trinity Southern University in Dallas, Texas, had awarded an M.B.A. to Colby Nolan—a Pennsylvania Assistant Attorney General's cat. After this revelation, officials in Texas took action against Trinity Southern University.

Just think of the implication of these statutes. If each state had such laws, and enforced them, this would seriously impede the growing market for fraudulent credentials. By eliminating the demand side, the supply side will dry up in time.

What can we do about this problem?

Like degree mills, accreditation mills like to operate in the dark, without a lot of fanfare. Very few have ever advertised their existence, other than having a Web site. Of course, the best way we can rid ourselves of this problem is through legislation, followed by enforcement. I see no national legislation on the horizon regarding either degree mills or accreditation mills, thus it is up to each state to police itself. If each state would pass legislation outlawing the manufacture, possession, and use of any type of educational credential (either counterfeit or just worthless), and forbid the use of any educational credential that is not issued by an institution accredited by an entity recognized by the U.S. Department of Education or CHEA, we would be farther ahead in this battle.

If you encounter an accreditation mill, obtain copies of its literature, Web site, requirements for accreditation, lists of their "accredited" members, etc. Now that you are armed with facts and evidence, consider contacting your State Attorney General, Consumer Protection Department, or your state

Table 1. Examples of Accreditation Mills

Accreditation Mill	"Accredited School"
American Council of Colleges and Universities	St. James University
American Council of Private Colleges and Universities	Hamilton University
Association for Online Academic Accreditation	
Association for Online Academic Excellence	
Association for Online Distance Learning	Almeda College and University
Association of Distance Learning Programs	International College of Homeland Security, Irish International University
Association of Private Colleges and Universities (formed by founder of Trinity College and University)	
Council for International Education Accreditation	Ashworth College
Council for National Academic Accreditation	Will accredit anyone for $1,850
Distance Graduation Accrediting Association	St. Regis University, Capitol University
Distance Learning Council of Europe	Wexford University
Educational Quality Accrediting Commission	Bircham Internationall University, American Coastline University, Irish International
European Committee for Home and Online Education	University of Dorchester, Dunham, Strassford, Shaftesbury, Stafford
European Council for Distance and Open Learning	Universityof Palmers Green, San Moritz, Harrington University
Higher Accreditation Services Association	Ellington, Lexington, Stanton University
International Accreditation Agency for Online Universities	Belford University
International Accrediting Commission for Postsecondary Institutions	Adam Smith University
International Accreditation Society	Southern Pacific University
International Commission for Excellence in Higher Education	Monticello University
International Commission for Higher Education (Accreditation Commission)	
International Distance Education and Training Council (IDETC)	American Central University
International Distance Learning Accreditation Council	Americus University
Midwestern States Accreditation Agency	American Western University
National Academy of Higher Education	Madison University, Concordia University— offers a degree in 12 hours
National Accreditation Association	American International University
National Association for Private Post Secondary Education	

Table 1. Examples of Accreditation Mills	
Accreditation Mill	**"Accredited School"**
National Association of Open Campus Colleges	Southwestern University
National Board of Education (NBOE)	St. Regis University
National Distance Learning Accreditation Council	Suffield College & University
New Millennium Accrediting Partnership for Educators Worldwide (NAPFEW)	U. of Berkley
North American College and University Accrediting Agency	
The American Bureau of Higher Education	Concordia College
United Nations Convivium for International Education	
United States Distance Education & Training Council	
West European Accrediting Society	Loyola, Lafayette, Cromwell University
Western Association of Schools and Colleges	Loyola, Roosevelt, Cromwell University
World Association of Universities and Colleges	American World University, Edison, Cambridge State University, and previously William Howard Taft University
World Online Education Accrediting Commission	Ashwood University
Worldwide Accrediting Commission	Loyola, Paris; DePaul

governing body regulating private postsecondary education. Also consider contacting a local investigative reporter (always looking for a juicy story), the education writer at your local newspaper, or a television investigative reporter. By bringing these criminal actions to the forefront, you can help eliminate them.

In 1983, two investigative reporters at *The Arizona Republic* newspaper (Richard Robertson and Jerry Seper) recognized that Arizona had a problem with degree mills. Their investigations resulted in a series of front page articles about the numerous degree mills which then operated from Arizona. To prove their point as to exactly how easy it was to set up a school, the two reporters incorporated their own school—the University of the Republic—and of course, also incorporated their own accrediting entity—Southwest Accrediting Commission. They then placed an advertisement in *The Washington Post* offering degrees for sale. In a short amount of time, and with less than $100, they formed both their university and accreditor. Then the reporters went public.

One of their stories, "Diploma Mills: A Festering Sore on Arizona Education," so embarrassed the state legislature, that new laws were passed in Arizona outlawing degree mills. The result was that Arizona degree mills either went out of business, or just moved next door to Utah.

Legitimate accreditation is extremely important, as the federal government renders its decisions about institutional and program eligibility for student financial aid and other federal grants. Thus, it is up to us to remain vigilant concerning accreditation mills, and to take action when they are observed. We must police our own profession. Take action and become a part of the solution.

◇◇◇◇◇◇◇◇◇◇◇◇◇◇◇◇

(Book Review)

Degree Mills: The Billion Dollar Industry That Has Sold Over a Million Fake Diplomas

BY ALLEN EZELL AND JOHN BEAR, PROMETHEUS BOOKS, AMHERST, NY. (2005). PAPERBACK: 318 PP.

Reviewed by Thomas D. Bazley, Ph.D.

While academia focuses on the great problems of the world and prepares students to address them, Allen Ezell and John Bear argue passionately, if not convincingly that the integrity of these noble efforts is being seriously undermined by a scourge they refer to as "degree mills." They contend that over the past decade the sale of fake degrees has become a billion dollar industry. With an average cost of $1,000 each, a million individuals could be falsely touting their educational credentials. These estimates should not be viewed as mere hyperbole; the authors speak from knowledge and experience. Allen Ezell is a retired FBI agent who specialized in degree fraud for a great part of his law enforcement career and continues to provide consulting services on this issue. John Bear is a well known educational consultant and author of books on higher education. He has also been an expert witness in degree fraud litigation.

In fact, Ezell and Bear suggest they might be understating the breadth of the problem because of the conservative approach they take in defining what they consider degree mills. They clearly and repeatedly acknowledge that evaluating educational programs is fraught with difficulties and complexities and they ultimately leave it to the reader's discretion to determine whether a school is a degree mill, an innovative educational institution, or something in between. However, even without the existence of any universally accepted definition for a degree mill, they do not shy away from offering their opinion in this respect. They describe a degree mill as an entity in which:

◆ Degree granting authority does not come from a generally accepted government agency;

◆ Procedures for granting credit for prior learning, and for determining the amount and quality of work done to earn a degree, do not meet generally accepted standards; and

◆ Those who make the decisions on credit and on the quantity and quality of work do not have the credentials, experience, or training typically associated with people performing these tasks.

It is within these parameters that Ezell and Bear provide a comprehensive and often disturbing discussion of the availability and use of fake degrees. They trace the history of degree mills from 700 A.D. to present, with emphasis on the relatively short period from about 1980 to 1991. It was during that time that Ezell, then an FBI Special Agent, headed an investigative effort aptly named "DipScam." As a result, Ezell is able to provide rich details about an array of characters who have been involved in peddling fake degrees. Most impressively, he was responsible for dismantling 40 degree mills and convicting 21 individuals for selling worthless degrees (many of whom, nevertheless, reaped huge sums of money before being caught).

The authors also credit the joint work of two Congressional committees during this period for highlighting the fake degree problem. Committee investigators were able to procure a fraudulent Ph.D. in psychology for one of the committee chairs, the late Claude Pepper. When the degree was presented to him at a Congressional hearing, he became "Dr. Pepper." (Note: At the time, the author of this article was a U. S. Postal Inspector and was temporarily assigned to Pepper's staff as an investigator. He was instrumental in making the undercover purchase of the degree. Subsequently, in his capacity as a U. S. Postal Inspector, he had occasional professional contacts with Allen Ezell.)

Aside from whatever distaste arises from hucksters financially benefiting from selling worthless degrees, Bear and Ezell provide compelling evidence of an even larger problem, i.e., the manner in which these degrees are being used by the purchasers. In an appendix appropriately titled "Time Bombs," the authors provide a thirteen page list of real-life scenarios in which individuals possessing unequivocally fraudulent degrees (per Ezell and Bear), have occupied or are currently in responsible professional positions that normally require bona fide academic credentials. Among these scenarios are individuals currently employed as faculty and administrators at colleges and universities. Although no individuals are identified by name, sufficient information is furnished to determine the accuracy of these allegations. For this reason alone, higher education executives may wish to peruse this volume.

However, beyond ferreting out employees with fictitious credentials, there are additional important steps these executives can and should take. In their final chapter, Ezell and Bear present a wide-ranging discussion of what can be done to curb degree fraud. Given Ezell's background, it is not surprising that a renewed law enforcement effort is among the recommendations. There certainly have been and probably will continue to be aggravated cases that warrant government intervention. Nevertheless, approaching the fraudulent degree problem from this perspective might be akin to addressing drug abuse solely from the supply side, i.e., simply focusing on the prosecution of the traffickers and dealers, a law enforcement strategy that has not met with resounding success. Fortunately, Ezell and Bear make recommendations that address the "demand" side of the equation as well. In general their recommendations in this regard seek to diminish the value of fraudulently obtained degrees and it is here that administrators and executives at institutions of higher learning can play a critical role. For instance, these officials are urged to exercise informed judgment in making decisions about accepting degrees and/or credits for admission purposes so that fake credentials are not honored. In addition, they call upon human resource professionals, including the federal government's own personnel agency, the Office of Personnel Management, to become more vigilant in accepting academic credentials for employment. If fraudulent degrees cannot be used to obtain further education at legitimate institutions or employment, the demand for these worthless credentials will subside.

Moreover, the authors call upon legitimate institutions of higher education to aggressively protect their good name. They provide several examples of degree mills copying or making slight modifications to names of renowned institutions of higher learning for the sole purpose of creating deception and confusion on the part of students and those who evaluate academic credentials for educational or employment purposes, thus adding value to these worthless documents.

The authors also urge state departments of education and the U.S. Department of Education to enact licensing standards for postsecondary educational institutions, which would limit the ability of degree mills to obtain any type of government agency approval. In part, they draw support for this recommendation from a doctoral dissertation entitled "Diploma Mills: What's the Attraction," authored by Robin J. Calote (2002, University of LaVerne). In this study, Calote found that purported licensure was the only statistically significant variable that influenced a group of students who were asked to choose among sixteen fictitious colleges for enrollment. Among her concluding remarks, she urged legitimate institutions to provide counseling to their students to educate them about academic accreditation, what state licensure and approval means, the existence and operation of diploma mills, and the professional risks taken by those who acquire and use fake degrees. In response to these recommendations Ezell and Bear state, "We could not agree more." And nor can I.

Thomas D. Bazley holds a Ph.D. in Criminology from the University of South Florida, Tampa. He served as U.S. Postal Inspector for nearly 27 years where he specialized in white collar crime investigations. He resides in Tampa, FL.

◇◇◇◇◇◇◇◇◇◇◇◇◇◇◇

Resources

Compiled by Ann M. Koenig

Degree Mills: The Billion-Dollar Industry that has Sold over a Million Fake Diplomas by Alan Ezell and John Bear, Prometheus Books, 2005—www.prometheusbooks.com and www.degreemills.com.

Information Resources Concerning Unaccredited Degree-Granting Institutions, compiled by George Gollin, Physics professor, University of Illinois at Urbana-Champaign: A compilation of various resources, including news items, and public legal documents—http://web.hep.uiuc.edu/home/g-gollin/pigeons/

Don't Judge a College by Its Internet Address, Chronicle of Higher Education, Nov. 26, 2004—http://chronicle.com/free/v51/i14/14a02901.htm

Special Report: Degrees of Suspicion published by Chronicle of Higher Education, June 25, 2004—http://chronicle.com/prm/weekly/v50/i42/42a00902.htm. Includes articles:
  ◆ *Inside the Multimillion-Dollar World of Diploma Mills; What's A Diploma Mill?*;
  ◆ *Psst. Wanna Buy a Ph.D.?*;
  ◆ *A Small World*;
  ◆ *Maxine Asher Has a Degree for You*;
  ◆ *The Hypnotist Who Married Lana Turner*;
  ◆ *The University of Spam*;
  ◆ *"Let Me Be Honest With You..."*; and
  ◆ *Tilting at Diploma Mills.*

Fact Sheet # 6: Important Questions about "Diploma Mills" and "Accreditation Mills," published by the Council for Higher Education Accreditation (CHEA)—www.chea.org/Research/C HEA%20Fact%20Sht%206%20Diploma%20Mills.pdf

Diploma Mills and Accreditation: U.S. Department of Education information on accreditation, diploma mills, and misrepresentation in the U.S. system of education—www.ed.gov/students/prep/college/diplomamills/index.html

U.S. Federal Trade Commission:
  ◆ *Avoid Fake Degree Burns by Researching Academic Credentials*—www.ftc.gov/bcp/conline/pubs/buspubs/diplomamills.htm
  ◆ *Degree Mills: Degrees of Deception*—www.ftc.gov/bcp/conline/pubs/alerts/diplomaalrt.htm

Degree.net Web site, by Ten Speed Press: Consumer-oriented articles on issues in higher education, including diploma mills and accreditation, presented by the publisher of the *Bears' Guides*—www.degree.net.

The *Bears' Guides,* published by Ten Speed Press: These guides to non-traditional education, written over the past 30 years, list many fake, substandard, and dubious institutions and accreditors. Available from the publisher (www.tenspeed.com) and many commercial booksellers. Older editions are sometimes available through used book Web sites.

Fraud and Education: The Worm in the Apple, by Harold J. Noah and Max A. Eckstein, Rowman & Littlefield Publisher, Inc., 2001.

Also by Allen Ezell, diploma mill expert and AACRAO presenter

"Are Current Safeguards Protecting Taxpayers Against Diploma Mills?" Testimony to the U.S. federal Committee on Education in the Workforce, Subcommittee on 21st Century Competitiveness—http://edworkforce.house.gov/hearings/108th/21st/dmills092304/wl092304.htm

Diploma Mills—Past, Present, and Future, published in College and University quarterly journal, Winter 2002—www.aacrao.org/publications/candu/index.cfm

By Alan Contreras, Oregon, Office of Degree Authorization

Diploma Mills, published by the Oregon Student Assistance Commission, Office of Degree Authorization—www.osac.state.or.us/oda/diploma_mill.html

A Case Study in Foreign Degree (Dis)approval, published in International Higher Education, Summer 2003—www.bc.edu/bc_org/avp/soe/cihe/newsletter/News32/text004.htm

International Diploma Mills Grow with the Internet, published in International Higher Education, Summer 2001—www.bc.edu/bc_org/avp/soe/cihe/newsletter/News24/text003.htm

How Reliable is National Approval of University Degrees?, published in International Higher Education, Fall 2002—www.bc.edu/bc_org/avp/soe/cihe/newsletter/News29/text005.htm

From Other Sources

Degree Duplicity by Mark Clayton, The Christian Science Monitor, June 10, 2003—www.csmonitor.com/2003/0610/p15s02-lehl.html

United States Government Accounting Office Purchases of Degrees from Diploma Mills—www.gao.gov/new.items/d03269r.pdf

Fake School Reveals Holes in Loan Program, CNN.com—www.cnn.com/2003/EDUCATION/01/21/fictitious.school.ap

Chairman Collins: Loophole Allows Taxpayer Dollars to Pay for Federal Workers' Diploma Mill Degrees. Urges Office of Personnel Management to Issue Regulations—www.senate.gov/~gov_affairs/072503presssc2.htm

Some International Approaches to Fighting Diploma Mill Fraud

Italy's Internet Dottores Risk Jail, published in the Times Higher Education Supplement—www.thes.co.uk/search/story.aspx?story_id=2024571

Japan: NHK-TV, public TV station in Japan, produced an episode of its program *"Gendai: Close Up"* on the topic of diploma mills, featuring a taping at the Diploma Mill Workshop at the AACRAO 2005 Annual Conference in New York City and interviews with Allen Ezell and George Gollin, and trips around the US to visit purported diploma mill operators. The program aired in Japan in Japanese—www.nhk.or.jp/english/index.html

Liberia: Ministry of Education Identifies Illegal Learning Institutions—www.analystnewspaper. com/moe_identifies_illegal_learning_institutions.htm

Government Finally Closes St. Luke [medical school]—http://allafrica.com/stories/ 200507200430.html

Netherlands: Ministry of Education, Culture, and Science launches Web site in July 2005 to inform educational institutions, employers and the general public about the program of diploma mill fraud—www.diplomamills.nl/zakelijk/Diplomamills/s10_algemeen.asp (in Dutch)

Sweden: Bluffuniversitet och falksa examsbevis—Sverige och världen (Fake Universities and Bogus Degrees—Sweden and the World) report published by the Swedish National Agency for Higher Education (in Swedish)—http://web2.hsv.se/publikationer/rapporter/2005/ 0525R.pdf; Summary in English—http://english.hsv.se/publications/reports/report/ ?contentId=2181

Off-shore medical schools: Chronicle of Higher Education International feature section on off-shore medical schools, levels of regulation of Caribbean medical schools, watchdog groups, maps (October 28, 2005)—http://chronicle.com/weekly/v52/i10/10a05501.htm. Includes:

- *Sun, Sand and an M.D.*;
- *Offshore Medical Schools Operate with Minimal Oversight*;
- *A Hissing Match on Bonaire*;
- *A Pioneering Offshore Medical School Gains Credibility*; and
- *The Egg Man and Other Anti-Fraud Activists.*

U.S. Accreditation

The six regional accrediting associations in the United States:

- Middle States Association of Colleges and Schools—www.msche.org/
- New England Association of Schools and Colleges—www.neasc.org/
- North Central Association of Colleges and Schools—www.ncahigherlearning commission.org/
- Northwest Association of Schools, Colleges and Universities—www.nwccu.org/
- Southern Association of Colleges and Schools—www.sacscoc.org/
- Western Association of Schools and Colleges—www.wascweb.org/

The two organizations in the U.S. that approve accrediting agencies:

- Council for Higher Education Accreditation (CHEA): See links "Degree Mills and Accreditation" and "Database of Institutions and Programs Accredited by Recognized U.S. Accrediting Organizations" on the CHEA home page—www.chea.org.
- U.S. Department of Education: Office of Postsecondary Education Database of Institutions and Programs Accredited by Agencies and State Approval Agencies Recognized by the U.S. Secretary of Education—http://ope.ed.gov/accreditation/; also Diploma Mills and Accreditation—www.ed.gov/students/prep/college/ diplomamills/index.html

AACRAO Transfer Credit Practices Online—www.aacrao.org/users_only/TCPForm/